The Wheels *of the* Bus
Go Round *and* Round

The Wheels *of the* Bus Go Round *and* Round

The life of a school bus driver

Dewey William Stedman

LIBERTY HILL PUBLISHING

Liberty Hill Publishing
555 Winderley Pl, Suite 225
Maitland, FL 32751
407.339.4217
www.libertyhillpublishing.com

Paperback ISBN-13: 978-1-6628-8693-5
Ebook ISBN-13: 978-1-6628-8694-2

Chapter Index

————— ⮞✳⮜ —————

Author's Note:

This book is the life story of a boy who was born right at the end of World War II, and born in Washington state near a U.S. Navy shipyard.

Chapter 1

Growing up in the Pacific Northwest

I was born in the hospital in Bremerton, Washington on 27 December 1944. My father worked in the shipyard and my oldest brother worked part of the day in the shipyard, then attended school classes part of the day. He made a career of working for the Dept. of the Navy on big ships needing repairs. He was mainly a pipe fitter. The house I grew up in was in a housing complex of government-built homes near Port Orchard. At the end of the war, this housing development closed down. My father and mother purchased one of the houses and moved it to five acres near there, then remodeled it into a nice home to grow up in. The house was on the front part of the five acres. As a kid, I had chores to do around home, such as feed the animals which we had over the years, including pigs, cows, and lots of chickens. I had to collect the eggs daily, and once a week or so, had to clean out the chicken house, which wasn't one of my favorite jobs. We had a small wood stove in the kitchen, plus an electric range. I had to help my dad, oldest brother, and a neighbor cut the trees down at the back of the property. The neighbor brought his tractor over to our house and dragged the trees to an area near the chicken house that was for wood for the winter, so it would be dry for burning in the kitchen. We would move the cut-up wood to the back porch and stack it, so my mother could use her little wood stove

1

for heat in the kitchen. We also had a stove oil heater in the living room to warm up the rest of the house. There were no vents in the house, so it would get cool in the night time. Getting all the wood hauled out of the woods, cut, and split was a lot of work. We didn't have a chainsaw in the early days, so we used a lot of ax work, and towed the long trees out of the woods. The neighbor had a big saw that he attached to the back of his tractor so it would make the pieces the size we needed, and I had to split and stack it in the shed. That took a lot of days and sweat.

In return for the neighbor helping us, we went over to his house, helped him cut his wood, and dragged it up to his house to cut it into the sizes he wanted. He had an old gray Ford tractor and I hung out at his house a lot; he trained me to drive the tractor. At first, I would drive it down his long driveway — since his house was quite a way off the road — to get his mail or newspaper. As my father's health started to fail him, and as I got older, I hauled the trees out of the woods at our house and his.

I want to go to school.

2

Our neighbor across the street also owned the gas station a block down the road from our house where I hung out a lot. They had three kids about my age, so we hung out together a lot. I spent a lot of time at their house, especially when my father got cancer of the throat and they removed his voice box. After the surgery, the smell of cancer was so bad that we had to keep some doors in the house closed all the time. He died on the last day of school when I was fifteen years old.

The gas station sold candy bars and other treats, so it was a hangout for me for many years. There were two other boys in the neighborhood, so we always would find something to do together. There was a pond out in woods where our brothers would hang out as kids. We found it, and would grab some food and go out there for lunch sometimes. When it got really cold, we would go out there and play our version of hockey. We would find a tree limb to use as a hockey stick and something to use as a puck. As country boys, we would find things to do.

A couple of times a year, we would put together a carnival with all kinds of games; throwing balls at bottles and a dart setup was popular. We would con the older people in the neighborhood to come, and we bought prizes and sold bags of popcorn. After paying for the prizes, we would divide the profits, if we had any. This neighbor had cows so we would go out into the pasture and turn over cow patties (manure), and look for worms. I had a big box at my house that we would put the worms into. When we got a lot of them, we would call the local fish bait shops and see if they wanted to buy them. We made a little money doing that. When the neighbors would go out of town for a few days, I would milk and feed the cows for them.

As kids, we did things like collecting beer and soda bottles. We would walk up and down the road, checking the ditches and grabbing all the bottles we could find. We would also peel the bark off cascara trees and sell it, and picked cones off of evergreen fir trees. We got a lot of money for a bag of cones. We also picked berries of different kinds, and sold them. I even picked brush to be used in floral arrangements at flower shops. It was a lot of work, but good money. Sometimes, I got hired to do yard work for people.

Who painted me blue?

I had a lot of fun in school when I wasn't working at the gas station. I was hired the day I turned 16. The owner was good to me and let me off when something was really important that I wanted to do. I was well-liked and when I graduated, I was selected as most likely to remain a bachelor, but I fooled them since I have been married fifty-six years now to the same woman. In high school, I took mostly business/office type classes. I got straight A's in typing and zero in conduct in that class, since the teacher didn't like all the joking around that I did. If she left the classroom, I would grab the microphone and start telling jokes. The room was really big and I got caught doing that a few times. I took shorthand writing class so I could be a secretary. I liked that class since I was the only boy in the class. When I needed a date for a dance or something, I would start asking at row one until I got a date.

In the summer between the ninth and tenth grades, the old neighbors who sold the gas station had moved away. They moved to eastern Washington and were living and working on a large orchard. They knew I needed money, so they invited me to come spend the summer with them. It was hard work, but every day after work, we went down to the Columbia River which was part of the orchard, and we'd go water skiing. We had two boats available most of the time. One Sunday afternoon, I lost my balance and ended up in the river. Thank God that there were only guys in the boat, since my swimsuit was around my ankles when they pulled me out of the water. They all laughed at me.

At the end of the summer, I took a lot of money home with me, and I went to Bremerton and bought a 1953 Ford convertible that a man was selling. I knew my mother wouldn't let me bring the car home so I parked it at my friend's house. We were like brothers, since our mothers had shared the same room in the hospital when we were born, and they liked me, so they let me park it there. As kids growing up, we hauled sleeping bags up and down the road all summer, sleeping at each other's houses in the backyard during the summer. I would walk up to his house, get my car, and run around. I then parked it there and walked home. It was less than a mile.

I decided I'd better get insurance on the car in case I got into a wreck. The only insurance man I knew was where my dad got his insurance, so I drove there to get a quote so I could save money to get it. Unfortunately, later that afternoon, my oldest brother ran across the insurance man and he asked my brother what he thought of my convertible. My brother said, "What convertible?" So, the insurance man told him about it. Needless to say, my brother came looking for me and made me put it up on blocks at this property at Southworth that he owned, and had a little plant nursery there. He let me have it back after I could pay six months insurance on it. It was one of the coolest cars at the high school. The girls all loved riding in it.

I always had a car full of kids in it, and we would cruise around town. If we got bored, we did stoplight stops, where everyone in the car would get out, run around the car, get back into it, and go when the light turned green. One night, a girl classmate who hung out with me a lot jumped out when the light turned red; she caught the pocket of her new coat on the chrome strip on the left front fender and ripped it. Her mother wasn't a happy camper with that happening, but still let her go out with me. After we graduated, she went to college and I ended up in Alaska. A classmate who had an old Ford two-door loved to play "car chase" around the streets of downtown Port Orchard. One night, I forgot what street I was on. I turned left onto the street which housed the police station. An officer was walking out the front door, saw what we were doing, and flagged us down. He made us go into the police station, gave us a verbal lecture, and let us go with no ticket.

One time, someone broke into a closed-down gas station, which was rented to a guy to store his full beer truck at night. They had no clue who did it until two students were in Bremerton, driving around and drinking beer. They threw a full beer out of the window to watch it roll down this steep street. An officer saw it, stopped them, and found several cases of beer in the truck. It happened to be the kind of beer that had been stolen. The boys admitted to stealing the beer. It was a whole pickup load of beer. They were hiding it out in the woods near a lake. The bad part was that the father of the boy with the truck ended up hauling it back to town in his car, since the truck was disabled.

I hate pink!

I don't like black paint

Chapter 2

Moving to Alaska after graduation

W ith no future plans after graduating, my brother mentioned that he maybe could get me a job in Alaska where he was working. A couple of months went by, and not hearing anything more about Alaska from my brother, I decided to go into the army. I went to the recruiting office in Bremerton and talked to them about joining. They gave me a ticket to take a ferry boat to Seattle, to have a physical and see if I qualified. When I got back from the recruiter in Bremerton, I checked the daily mail, and there was a letter from my brother with an airline ticket to Fairbanks, Alaska for the next week. I got into the car and took the ferry ticket back to the army recruiter, and told him, "Thanks, but I have new plans."

I packed my bag, and off to Alaska I went, only eighteen-years-old, and with no clue of what was going to happen or what kind of job I would be doing. The job was at Clear Air Force base, working for R.C.A., which was the contractor who operated the Ballistic Missile Early Warning System for the air force defense systems. My job was a secretary in a small department, which consisted of my boss and me. Our mission was to control all the panels needed to build a round radar enclosure for the new revolving radar system being built. It looked like a giant golf ball. The rest of the equipment there involved three antennas. Each was the size of a football field on edge, standing up length-wise, aimed toward Russia, as this was during the Cold War era.

Most evenings after dinner, my boss and I would end up in the club room, where there were pool tables, shuffleboards, and a lounge to have a beverage of your choice, just relaxing and visiting with other employees. My boss and I loved to play shuffleboard, so most nights we did that. One night while we were playing, three young girls walked by us and sat down in the lounge area. It was the first time to see girls close to my age. My boss asked me if I was going to continue playing or go visit the girls since I had lost all desire to continue the game. We stopped playing.

I went over and started talking to the girls, and found out that one was only two years younger than me. They had moved in with their sister's family on a homestead near the base. Their father was going to do car maintenance for local people at the homestead. The girls were going to school in Nenana, and the bus picked them up and dropped them off at the base daily. I started asking the older one (who is now my wife) out on dates. I was able to borrow cars from friends to take her to a movie or out to dinner. I would call her mother on the local citizens band radio for a date, since cell phones weren't developed yet. Everybody who had their radio would hear me. Sometimes, the bus driver would tell her where she was going with me that night.

Please buy me. I miss the kids.

Realizing that I needed a car and the site's doctor was going back to the States, I bought his 1962 red Impala so that I had something to run around in. The government started drafting people into the army, so a guy my age and I went to Fairbanks and joined an army reserve unit. We joined on the buddy plan, so we got to do basic training together. I sold my car and we thought we were going for training in California. They got hold of me at my mother's house, which we stopped at on the way, and they changed our orders for us to go to Fort Leonard Wood U.S. Army base which is in Missouri. I had sent money to a car dealer in Portland, Oregon, so we went to get it. I figured I could find somewhere off the base to store it during basic training.

When we got to the dealership, he had sold it, and wouldn't give me my money back. An army lawyer went after him, and I got my money back after I got to the fort. We walked down the road and found an old Plymouth station wagon cheap, so I bought it. While driving through Idaho at about six in the morning, with the sun in my eyes, the road made a sharp turn and I ended up smashing into a car head on. We both got taken to the hospital. I had bruised joints from the waist up. My friend got a cut above his eyebrows, and got banged up pretty good. We didn't have enough money to buy another car so I contacted the fort about what had happened, and they wired us bus tickets to get to the fort.

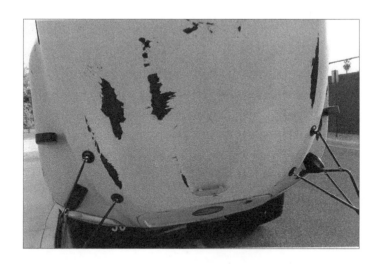

Please paint me

Another problem was that we had shipped our army clothes to a friend in California where we were going to stay for a few days before starting training. They gave us a few clothes until our army bags got to us. It got really cold there in the winter, so they asked anybody if they had frostbite before. I had both ear tops frozen, so they put white stripes on both shoulder straps of my coat which exempted me from training outside in freezing weather. I looked like a lieutenant, so most everybody would salute me, and I would return the salute. It was fun while it lasted.

After a few weeks, we were able to go to the club and have a beer. We had a group of true Alaskans that hung out together. They would go to the club most nights. When they would get back, the smallest of them would be very drunk and pass out, so we would put him in his bed and move the bed to different places around the barracks, such as the shower room, outside in the bushes, or, the best time was when we put him and his bed on top of the pool table. At the end of basic training, he got sent to California, to a small base for training in his new job skill. We both held the title of Personal Specialist. I got to stay at Fort Leonard Wood.

We had a lot of fun guys in our class, and on weekends, we would hop a bus, go to different cities in Missouri, and drink a little beer. You had to pass your test for the week to get a pass to go. One week I didn't, but I went with the group to a city where there were two all-girl colleges. I would sneak in and go to the bathroom, and they would get me a drink. One time, they were checking identification for legal age inside the door, so I stayed outside and one guy got a stamp with a lot of ink. He came outside and we transferred as much of the ink over to my hand. We did a good enough job that I was flagged through. On the way back, I was hoping that they weren't going to do an inspection of the bus to make sure everyone had an off-base pass.

I was happy that they didn't check our bus, but thirty minutes later, there was a robbery on base and the base got shut down for several hours. I only failed one week of the eight.

Before we left Alaska, and while at Fort Leonard Wood, a co-worker told me that I needed to visit his father who was one of the big officers on base. He was a "Full Bird Colonel". His next promotion would be to General. The first day in school they told us that we would not get phone calls during the day. About the third day, an office clerk came into our class asking for a Private Stedman. I raised my hand and he told me to follow him to the company office.

He had me sit in the office of our company leader and dialed my friend's dad. He welcomed me to the fort and asked if I would like to come to his house on Sunday for dinner and to watch some football. Of course, I said yes, and he told me what time he was going to pick me up. He arrived in his car, which had officers' stickers on it, and everyone saluted him. We had a great dinner and watched a lot of football. As we were leaving to return to the barracks, his wife gave me two pieces of pie on paper plates. A couple of weeks later, I was asked over again, but was told to catch a base cab since I knew what his house address was. I got into the cab and the driver refused to take me to his house, so I told him to take me to a base police station, which he did. I explained what was going on and after they called him, the cab took me to dinner. A few days later, he called me to ask to borrow my Alaskan pictures to show his daughter who was visiting. He said he would be there at about 5:00 p.m., which was mail time at the orderly room. He showed up and the first sergeant called everyone to order (to line up in rows), and he went back to the full bird and saluted him. He called my name to come to the rear. I saluted the officer and in a very low voice, he asked me how everything was going, and I told him great. I reached into my back pocket, got the pictures out, gave them to him, and saluted him as he walked away. That really stirred up the pot. I never had a bad detail assigned to me. I guessed if you knew the right person, good things happened. We both got back to Clear Air Force base from playing soldier. After a couple army drill meetings in Fairbanks, the United States Secretary of Defense decided to close eighty different military units, including ours. Everyone in the unit was put into an army manpower pool in St. Louis, Missouri, until their contract was up.

The first house that Ruth's family lived in in Fairbanks was owned by a catholic hospital next door. Her mother and her and her sister got part-time jobs there. They let me sleep on the floor in the living room when I went to town to date her, since they liked me.

My tonsils started bothering me, and the base doctor where I worked said that they needed to be removed; they got me an appointment with a doctor in Fairbanks. After the surgery, my girlfriend's mother asked me if I wanted to stay at their house to heal up before going back to Clear Air Force base, where I worked, since the doctor said I had to stay in town for a week, so he was planning on me staying in the hospital. I asked him if I could stay next door in that little house. My girlfriend assured him her mother approved, and it was verified since she worked down in the kitchen. That was an interesting hospital since to get to the operating room, they had to wheel you through the edge of the kitchen on the gurney. As they wheeled me through there, I waved to everyone I knew, but I was in "La La Land" when taken to the hospital room after surgery.

On the base, if you were eighteen, you could drink beer and the bars in the areas off-base didn't care. If your head was above the top of the bar, they would serve you, and if it wasn't, they had a stool for you to sit on. One time, they had a party when the sewer system at a local trailer park thawed out. It was a big thing, as only one trailer had a bathroom that worked, and the people living there let people come in through the back door, but everyone had to go to the base to shower. It was held at a local bar made of logs, with a big fireplace inside. It had peeled log beams running across the inside, and if you could jump up, and climb over the top, the management would give you a case of beer, for one time only. One guy could do it in twelve seconds, so he would challenge guys that he could do it faster than them for drinks, for *everyone* in the bar. I got a lot of free drinks, but I couldn't do it. I loved watching these big airmen or contractors with big mouths get beat time-after-time. The party for the thawing out was fun since they put in a new toilet with a stopper plug in it. It was filled full of spiked juice. The toilet seat had a fir muff attached to it, and you had to take the dipper and reach into the toilet to get a drink. When a state trooper would stop by there for coffee, I would go out to my car until he left. If I had my girlfriend with me, she would hide in the car with me.

Chapter 3

Living in the outback of Alaska

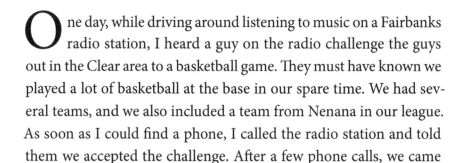

One day, while driving around listening to music on a Fairbanks radio station, I heard a guy on the radio challenge the guys out in the Clear area to a basketball game. They must have known we played a lot of basketball at the base in our spare time. We had several teams, and we also included a team from Nenana in our league. As soon as I could find a phone, I called the radio station and told them we accepted the challenge. After a few phone calls, we came up with a date for the game. With the help of my girlfriend and her family, we were able to make this happen.

A lot of people from the Clear Air Force base area wanted to go, so I called the bus company, which made daily trips to the base from Fairbanks to hire a bus for people to go to the game. I got my girlfriend to find a printer to make up some tickets to sell. The radio station was promoting the game. We came up with the idea of selling raffle tickets for three different gifts. With the game set for April Fool's Day, we had to put a little excitement into the game. I bought a nice tapestry for third prize. I bought a nice toaster for second place, and first place was a washer and dryer. Since it was April Fool's Day, the washer was a metal two-inch washer, and the dryer was a roll of paper towels. Everybody got a lot of laughs and nobody complained.

We made it a point that everybody had to wear a costume. The radio guys dressed mostly like aliens, and we dressed like farm people. Our center was only four feet, six inches, and only wore a diaper. We had Farmer John and lots of other crazy outfits. I was the center's mother, so I wore a blond wig with makeup. I borrowed a nursing bra and put a grapefruit in each cup. I wore a garter belt with one nylon painted red, and the other was green. I had real large panties on, with a rose design on each leg. I came out of the dressing room with an old pink baggy robe on and right before start of the game, everyone got to see what I was actually wearing. During the game, there were a few times that a grapefruit fell out and I'd pretend to hide, and put it back into the bra. Near the end of the game, I threw it up into the stands and people threw it back to me. We all acted crazy out on the floor, and a lot of the people were there to support the radio station. The stands were full of cheering people. We had chosen to give our share of the profit to the Lions CARE project, which was very popular at the time. The radio station gave us their share to go to the same project. The bus company didn't charge us. The school district didn't charge us. The printed tickets were free. I was given a Lions' special award, since they had said there was enough money to feed 500 people for thirty days with our money. I gave thanks to my girlfriend and her family for all the help they had done.

I want to be yellow again.

The base would have Green Time parties every time the record would get broken for a new length of time for not being broke down and off line. I was able to go to two of these parties while working at the base. They would put on a big special dinner. One time, they sent people to Fairbanks, looking for women to come out on a train and dance with the men. That was a fun party.

On the day of the big earthquake in April 1964, I was driving out to the homestead in my car, and it was sliding all over the road. It didn't look that slick out. When I arrived at my girlfriend's place everyone was outside in the yard. I asked them why they were out in the yard with no coats on. They said, "Look over toward those tall trees." They were moving really hard, back and forth, and I could feel the ground moving. After it was over, she and I hopped into the car, and went to our favorite place down by the river to swap a few kisses on a bridge that wasn't completed. While there, we saw a vehicle driving down the railroad tracks next to where we were parked. They were inspecting the tracks since trains went back and forth from Anchorage to Fairbanks. When I got back to the base, we found out the new site doctor was having a beer when the earthquake happened, and the hanging lights started swinging like mad. He thought it was the Alaskan beer.

Two weeks later, four of us rented a small plane and flew to Anchorage, which had a lot of damage. Two of the guys had pilot licenses. We found out that some of the buildings had sunk into the ground downtown, and in one area, the whole hillside slid into the area called Cooks Bay. Lots of homes went into the water and lots of people lost their lives. There were lots of big cracks in the ground all over town. On one house, the whole front yard had sunk to the level of the basement floor, and the backyard hadn't moved at all. On one street downtown, one side wasn't damaged, but the other side had sunken down to the point that the large movie theater sign was laying on the street in a vertical position.

Getting to the base, you would drive sixty miles to Nenana, which was a small town on the Tanana River where one could take a barge with a paddle wheel tug attached to it to get across the river in the summer months. When it got cold and the river would start freezing up, you would then drive across the river on the ice until spring when it would melt, and the barge would start up again. It was fun doing spin outs on the ice on the river. The only way to get to town would be to flag down the train coming from Anchorage, or catch a ride on an airplane. I made a deal with a guy with a plane that I would leave my car in town at the airport and he could use it until the ice broke. I would go to Fairbanks at least once per week to see my girlfriend.

When it was getting close to her graduating from high school, I proposed to her and she accepted, so we decided to get married two days after she graduated. The week before the wedding, the river was still frozen. I grabbed my big suitcase and went to the airport to fly into Fairbanks, which I did every Saturday night after work. When I got to our local airport, the man who I always had flown with told me he had no seat for me. My hospital brother and a couple other friends grabbed me and told me they were kidnapping me for one last party with the boys. They assured me they had a ticket on the next morning commercial plane, so I said, "Well, let's party."

The next morning, the weather was really nasty and the commercial flight was canceled. I needed to get to Fairbanks with the suitcase and do some other things. They got hold of a private pilot who agreed to fly me after he took someone from Healy to Fairbanks. The only problem was that when he landed in Fairbanks, the airport wouldn't let him leave to come and get me. I called my girlfriend and told her what was happening. Her sister's boyfriend agreed to drive out and pick me up on the road across the river. I grabbed the suitcase, walked across the railroad bridge, and made it to the road to be picked up. The bridge was one of the longest bridges in Alaska.

Well, while standing on the road with snow coming down, a car came down the road and went by me. Five minutes later, they came back and picked me up. It was her sister's boyfriend, wife-to-be, and sister. As we headed the sixty miles to Fairbanks, we had a flat tire on the Corvair that we were in. Ron had a spare tire, but no jack. I saw a small tree that had been cut down so I went and got it. He had a five-gallon steel gas can, so I used it to pry the car off the ground and we got the tire changed. He was mad at me since I had bent his car fender a little.

The wedding went pretty well, except the minister wouldn't let us kiss in the service after being pronounced married. We were told to just rub noses. We have always laughed about it, and it was a good thing that we didn't get sniffles. I had my hospital brother help me find a place to hide the car, since I didn't want it messed up with writing, etc. He made it a point to drive us really slow from the church so nobody would get lost. I took off down the road at a fast speed to get rid of everybody. My father-in-law tried to catch up with me and he got stopped by a policeman. The youngest sister cried to the officer that we had gotten away. He felt sorry, so didn't give him a ticket if he would go back to town.

After spending a week on a honeymoon in Anchorage, we returned to normal life and got an apartment in a small community near the base. I taught Ruth how to drive my 1965 Chevy Impala, painted yellow with a four-speed in it. My friends called it the "yellow coffin" since they *knew* I was going to kill myself in it. The area's state trooper gave her the test. He had her parallel park the car in front of his house, with his personal car in front and police car behind. He left her lots of room, so she wouldn't hit either car.

Chapter 4

Promoted to the Bahamas

———————◆ ◡✳◠ ◆———————

About three months after getting married, I received a call from an RCA management person who said he was on Andros Island in the Bahamas. He told me he wanted me to come down there and run the department dealing with classified documents on the project, and start a technical library for the engineers, from scratch. He figured that working in central files at Clear, and knowing the rules for handling classified documents, I would be a good choice. He said RCA would pay our cost of shipping all our belongings, and all airplane charges and food on the way. I agreed, and ten days later, everything we owned, minus a few clothes, was in wood crates for shipping. I found a buyer for my car. A couple of years ago, I asked my friend who I had gone into the army with if my old car, which was a 65 Chevy Impala, was still in the area. He said it had a blown engine and it wasn't for sale. A year later, I bugged him some more, and he finally went and talked to the guy; he was told he had just sold it to someone in Fairbanks. I wasn't a happy person, since I really wanted my car back.

On the day we were flying out of Fairbanks, it was snowing really hard and the airport was shut down. We were bussed to a local air force base, where we got on our plane, heading toward Florida. After arriving and getting our bags in Florida, I called for a taxi. We moved our bags out to the street so we could see the taxi coming. All of a sudden, a couple came toward us. It ended up that Don had been a big department manager at Clear and we knew each other very well. They had been to the airport for dinner, and to watch planes come in and fly out. They asked us to come to their house with them for snacks and drinks before we went to the motel that had been reserved for us. The next morning, I got the rental car they had ordered for me so I could get a few little things done, and to check in at the headquarters for the RCA project I was going to be working on. While driving around, we saw this Ford car with Alaskan license plates in this grocery parking lot. It looked like another friend's car, so we went into the store and found Bill and Maxine. We ended up eating with them a couple of times. The reason they had moved down there was for work, and they were tired of the cold. They kept saying our marriage wouldn't last three years, since they knew I liked to party. Their marriage didn't even last *one* year after they got to Florida. Maxine remarried and had a good marriage until they both passed away. There we were, with no swimming suits, heading to the islands so we started stopping at clothing shops. We found one shop that had three boxes of suits in the back room, and they let us each buy one suit.

When I took control of all of the classified documents, I put them in my vault in my office. The guy that had been in charge had to sign for everything that he wanted. He considered me as merely a clerk and told me that because my wife wasn't working on the base, she was refused on base housing. I had a secretary working for me, so I was really management. For that reason, I had to take my wife to Nassau and find her a place to live until I located somewhere we could rent off-base. I found a two-bedroom duplex, and a couple to share it with and split the cost. It worked out well until the wife of the other couple got pregnant and had to go back to the States. That was the policy on this project, as our medical staff wasn't set up to work with pregnant women. About the time she left, a little cottage in the village came open, which used to be where the hotel cook lived, and we rented it from the hotel. The cottage was so small that the bedroom was half of the building with a bathroom, closet, living room, and kitchen in the rest of house. The stove in the kitchen was so small that it only had two burners, and if we used the oven, we had to keep turning the food around to get it to fully cook. It had coconut-bearing palm trees in the front yard. At Christmas time, I attached cardboard snowmen to the trees, and the local people asked what the stuff attached to the trees was. This cottage was really close to the beach so we did a lot of beach walking, and I bought an eight-foot sailboat to play in the ocean with. They ran shuttle vans to where we lived, since a few people lived in the hotel. One side of the hotel was along Fresh Creek, with a little sixteen-foot open boat and a small outboard so we could go across Fresh Creek to eat and drink at a Bahamian bar and grill. You could also walk about a mile up a little road from the ferry landing to a diving resort, which also served good food.

We had a snack bar, theater, and shop to buy little personal items, such as beer, soda, and healthcare items on the base. They had a great mess hall for eating. For those living off base, we would get a four-teen-page list of food items that we could buy, which would come by barge every other week. We really had to watch the size we were ordering. My wife wanted some red food coloring. When it came in, it was a quart bottle. We got lots of laughs on that.

Every year, red land crabs came out of the coral cracks on the island and headed to the beach to lay eggs. You would see hundreds of them at a time. They would climb up the screen doors on buildings. One morning, when I started up the 55 Chevy I had bought from our friend when he and his wife returned to the states, I heard a loud noise coming from the engine area. I lifted the hood and there were four crabs on the engine block. One of them was on top of the generator and was trying to catch the fan blades. I turned the motor off and tried to get the crabs, but they went down onto the transmission area. As we pulled out to go to work, we heard a crunching noise and I looked in the mirror to see four dead, squished crabs. If I came upon a large group of them blocking the road on the way to the base, my wife would get out and shoo them out of the way, so I could drive thru them. If you didn't do that, they would put their pinchers up in the air and puncture your tires.

With all the crabs running around, several of us would go out in the dark and catch every male crab we could find. We did this for several nights. We had a huge cardboard box that we would put them into, with pans of water and a bunch of lettuce to keep them alive. We would let everyone know we were having a beach party. The mess hall would bring food down. Guys would break off the large arm of the crab, and cut the points off arms. The crabs would be released in the area where we found them. They could eat with the small arm and would grow a new large arm. We had a new metal garbage can and the shop people made a rack we put into the can, so crabs would cook in the water we put in them with seasoning. We would set up a volleyball net and cut the tops of a bunch of green young coconuts and use them as our drinking cups at the party. The mess hall would bring an eight-gallon cooking pot out with it about half full of juice. Some people would bring some joy juice and put it in the pot. We called it (Kick-A-Pooh Juice), and we ate lots of crab. I had a couple of guys down range at one of the test sites who liked to dive that I could buy lobster tails from for fifty cents each. They would send them up to me on the helicopter when it stopped at their site.

Type of transportation on the base

This base was a venture between the United States Navy and the British Navy. They installed equipment on the ocean floor to detect different noises that ships made. The goal was for all ships to sound the same so submarines would have to surface to see who and what was above them. Sometimes, we would have foreign boats trying to get our secrets during test. The deck would open up and big antennas would come up into the air. We would send our plane up with a camera, take pictures, and let them know we knew they were there. We were told not to talk about the base and how big it was. Would you believe this: the Miami Herald newspaper did a big article about it and wrote about how many people worked there.

When we did a test, the data taken would be put on a copter, and security would bring it to my office where I would then process it into my logs. I would stamp it "Secret," or whatever it was rated. I was cleared to handle "top secret" if I needed it. The guard would take me to the airport where a plane was ready to take me to the navy base in Orlando, where the navy would sign for the data. I was finished for the day and the pilot would ask me where I wanted to go. Most of the time, I would go to Melbourne, but one time I went to Miami. The next day, I looked for a shipping company to haul some personal cars to the island for some of the employees. I found a boat; we had twenty-two cars delivered to the island and I was considered a hero.

I enjoyed going up and down the island. My wife liked to go on the copters on Saturdays to deliver the personal mail and papers. Sometimes, we would see big sharks. The hammerhead sharks were the neatest to see.

At one site, there was an electronic tech who I worked with in Alaska. When he left there, I told him I would see him in the Bahamas. I didn't know I would be sent down there. He was really shocked when I walked into the building where he was working down site. When he left for the States to work at Goddard Space Center in Greenbelt, Maryland, I had said, "See you at Goddard," but at that time, I didn't know I was going to be offered a job there. When I sent out a resume throughout RCA, I got a call from Goddard and shocked the heck out of him when I located where he lived, and my wife and I showed up at his door. After fifty years, we were still the best of friends with he and his wife. We also had another couple who got married while working on the island. The six of us did a lot of things together, and we were known as the "six amigos." The other couple lived in North Carolina.

While living in the small cottage in the village and hanging around the boat docks, I became good friends with a guy who had a fifty-seven-foot pleasure boat he lived on. One day, he asked me if I could help him take the boat to Nassau to have some repairs done on it. He steered it out into the ocean and turned the steering of the boat over to me. He told me what course to steer it on and disappeared, but would show up once in a while to make sure I was going in the direction he wanted to go. We had plenty of beverages for the trip and lots of snack food. He had a sign above the pilot area which read, "The skipper of the boat is authorized to perform marriages for the duration of the trip," and he did many of them while I hung around him. When we got to the dock where the boat was being repaired and got tied up, he unloaded a small motorcycle off of the boat, and we climbed on it to go to the airport. There, he would chain it up, put padlocks on it, and we would fly back to Andros. Usually, about a week later, we would do this trip, but in reverse. I made this trip with him several times.

Chapter 5

The Fate of the Moon River

➤ ➤※⋐ ◄

O ur first wedding anniversary was coming up, and I suggested we get a boat of our own to run around the island. After looking in the Miami Herald newspaper, I found a twenty-five foot for sale at a reasonable price, so I called him and set up a time to see it. We flew to Miami and took a ride up and down the local waterway for several miles, and it had everything I needed so I bought it.

I had talked to the guy with the boat near the base to see if he would help me bring it out to the island. He agreed and so we set up a date to do this.

He was planning on buying two small outboard motors for his little boat, and this would save him from shipping them, plus, he had other items that he wanted to get. We found a welding shop and had them build a steel rack to hang on the back of the boat, with one of the outboard motors on it so that if the main motor stopped, we could continue our trip with an outboard.

It was Saturday morning and the boat was loaded with everything we needed, and lots of food and drinks for the trip. We headed out into the ocean toward the Bahamas. We took turns steering the boat, and about 4:00 p.m., the big motor stopped running. We checked everything we could, but couldn't get it running, so we tried to start the outboard. After a while of pulling the starter cord, we decided it was time to get on the radio and call the coast guard for help. We asked them if they could find a boat which would tow us into Bimini Island, which was a small island on the way to Andros. We figured we would leave it there and come back with the big boat, then tow it to Fresh Creek. The coast guard couldn't get anybody to come out and get us, and all of a sudden, the transmission part of our radio quit. At that point, all we could do was listen to them. They were concerned that we had sunk. All of a sudden, a twenty-foot speed boat came up to us. We asked them to tow us in, but they said they didn't have time. All of a sudden, they asked us which way to Florida, and away they went. Shortly thereafter, we spotted about a fifty-foot boat coming toward us. We asked them to tow us in; they said they didn't have time, but would take us back to Florida, so we threw them a tow rope. They called the coast guard and informed them that they had us and our transmission was not working. They didn't tell them that it was radio problems. They started towing us, and the next thing they did was put out their fishing outriggers, so we sat on the back area of our boat, with fishing lines on both sides of us, all the way to Fort Lauderdale. When we got close to a boat dock that did repairs, they unhooked the rope, threw it back to us, and took off since they didn't want to have to declare us with the customs people.

During the week, I got a call that the motor and radio repairs were done so we could come and get it. On Saturday, my boat friend and I flew to Florida to pick up the boat. It started up well, and the radio was working well, so we worked our way out into the main ocean, heading for Andros Island, but we didn't make it an hour and the main motor stopped running, and again, we couldn't get the outboard motor started. We didn't realize we were crossing the main shipping lane for big ships, until we saw one coming toward us. We had our running lights on, but we didn't think they saw this twenty-five-foot boat so close to them. I got out our flare gun, loaded it, and shot a flare into the sky, and it landed on the deck of the ship. We were less than 100 feet from the side of the ship as it went by us. Now that our hearts had settled down, we decided it was time for us to call out a May Day on the radio. We told the coast guard where we were, and a coast guard reserve boat came out and towed us back to the boat yard to have it worked on again.

My friend told me he couldn't help me anymore because of the tax-free days that we had to watch, so the next trip would be by myself. The next Saturday, I headed out by myself in the dark. It was running really well, until about 1:00 p.m. when it stopped again, and yep, the outboard wouldn't start either. I called the coast guard, and they sent a plane to verify where I was. They had me put the orange blanket I had on the bow deck, and a few hours later, the boat was being towed again back to the place where I started that morning. I hopped the plane back to the island.

Being young and not using common sense, I should have sold it for what I could get out of it. After talking about it with my wife, we decided to give it one last try, but she insisted to come with me. She said that if I died out at sea, she wanted to be with me. I would say she loved me. My friend offered to let me take the navigational equipment so I would know where I was. I had charts on the boat for the trip. We flew to Florida, picked up the boat, and headed toward Andros Island. Everything was going great until about 4:00 p.m. and the motor stopped running *again*. The good news was that I was able to start the outboard motor. The outboard had no throttle bar to steer or speed control. I had to sit on top of the motor, facing backward. I steered the boat by turning my body, which would turn the motor. At the same time, I would have my right arm down on the motor holding the speed control lever in the fast position. My wife sat at the steering wheel and steered it in the direction we needed to go in. The winds started coming up, and the waves got worse, but we thought we were gaining a little. As it started to get dark, we could see a light in the direction we were going, which made us happy. The bad part was that the wind increased and lightning started up, so we couldn't get hold of the coast guard. I was really getting tired, so about midnight, we decided to call it a night as we couldn't see the white light any more. I almost fell into the water a couple of times, and it was getting harder and harder to keep my feet on the rack that the motor was on.

The boat had two little beds mounted on the side in the galley area, so we laid down. My wife took the top bunk, and when she woke up, the sea was calm, and as she looked out the window, all she could see was blue. At first, she felt we had sunk, and she was in Heaven, but then she really woke up and was happy. I got the navigation equipment out and found out that we had drifted into the Bermuda Triangle, where lots of ships and planes have disappeared during bad storms. I got hold of the coast guard and told them where we were and that we needed to be towed to land somewhere.

After many calls by the coast guard for someone to help us, we got a call from a boat who said they were going to come get us. About an hour after their first call, they called again, asking the size and color of our boat. I responded, telling them twenty-five feet long, with a white cabin and blue stripe. I asked them their description, and they answered they were an eighty-foot large tug boat, all gray. Eventually, they arrived and towed us to Freeport, Grand Bahama Island.

We were taken into the dock area, where big ships tied up. A guy on the dock tied up my bow rope. He realized how far it was down to our bow, so he went and got an extension ladder, and we were able to get on shore. We found a place to get a meal and a room for the night. Worried about all the expenses, we ordered the cheapest meal, which was spaghetti. My wife looked at me and said, "I'm so glad to be alive I'm going to order me a strawberry frozen drink to celebrate."

I said, "Me too!"

The next morning, I got a phone number where I could take the boat and store it, until we figured out what we were going to do next.

It came time to move the boat to the boatyard that I had spoken with, which was a couple of miles down the island. We climbed down onto the boat, and I got the outboard started. I called on the radio, "Freeport harbor control, this is the Moon River," and they answered. I told them I was leaving the harbor under outboard power. They gave me permission, so I climbed onto the outboard, my wife grabbed the steering wheel, and we moved the boat out of the harbor and into the ocean. While going by the harbor control tower, everybody up there was outside watching us with binoculars.

We made it down the island okay and tied it up. I called a cab and we put both outboards and other personal items we wanted to keep into the cab, and flew over to Andros where we lived.

It was great to be back on the island, and our friends were happy to see us. The story about our boat trip spread all over the base, and my boat friend Bill, couldn't find time to go get it with his boat. A fellow employee asked me if he could buy the boat since he wanted one down on the island, and he knew what was wrong and could fix it. The next weekend, he went over to Freeport, repaired it, and said it was running really well. The next Saturday, he hopped onto the commercial plane and flew to Freeport to bring the boat over to Andros, but didn't clear the trip with anybody or tell me.

About 5:00 p.m., a jeep from the base harbor security office showed up at my door telling me what he was doing, and wanted me to come down to their office to help them figure out where he could be. I grabbed the microphone and called Nickles town harbor control. When they responded, I asked them if they had seen the Moon River pleasure boat or heard from it, since that was a place he would have to stop at for fuel and maybe spend the night.

All of a sudden, we got a message from the captain of an Italian cargo ship that they had seen the boat, and the guy who bought it from me. We asked him where he was so maybe we could find someone to meet the ship and rescue the boat, and the base employee who bought it. We started checking around to see if we could find a fast boat to catch up with them, but got no response to our call. All of a sudden, the ship got a call from a village leader on one of the small islands that the ship would have to go by on its way to Italy. We listened to them setting up the meeting time. Unfortunately, the guy on the island didn't understand the time, and wasn't at the meeting position. The captain looked for him, and so he had to take the Moon River skipper to Italy. They chopped holes in the bottom of the boat and dumped it overboard into the ocean to sink to the bottom. With the amount of gas that was aboard, they couldn't chance having a fire on the cargo ship.

I was able to talk to the guy who owned the Moon River one last time, so I wished him a good trip to Italy. When he got there, he only had the clothes he was wearing. It was winter there, and he had no passport or any other papers to go on shore. The ship captain called the United States foreign office, and a guy got him some clothes and a permit to go onto shore. He was given an option of going back to Florida on the same ship, or deposit $2,000 into a certain bank in Florida, and they would get him the plane tickets to fly back to

Andros. He chose that option and was gone about two weeks. He also didn't finish paying me off for the purchase of the boat. He left the base a couple of months later. That ended our dreams of having a boat on the island.

I wanted to be a school bus.

I had a good time helping my boat friend Bill, at Fresh Creek. One day, we were out on his little ten-foot fiberglass boat in the harbor where his big boat was. All of a sudden, we noticed a big old wooden boat being towed; the guy towing it made a turn, causing the wooden boat to swing into a path that we couldn't get out of the way from. I was sitting on the front deck area of the little boat. The boat crashed into the middle of the bow and damaged some of the bow. It threw me to the stern of our boat. He continued towing the boat to the other side of Fresh Creek and tied it off, then disappeared into the village. My friend let me off and went across the creek and found the local police there, and told him what this guy did and how he had run away. After seeing the damage that was done to my friend's little boat, The officer said, "I know who did it."

My friend Bill filed papers to take him to court and get paid for the damage.

Going to court in this village on the island was very interesting. The trial was in a building where the locals' mailboxes were. If someone was involved in the case, he or she had to stand out in the street until they were called, in order to give information to the judge. After that, one could sit and listen to what people were offering. One young fisherman who I was friends with saw what had happened and he got called into the building. He pointed at me and told them, "Dually was in the bow and the boat hit my friends and did some damage." He always called me that name, and the good news was that my friend was awarded the money he asked for to make the repairs.

We were always looking for something to do to kill time. Sometimes, they would schedule trips to Nassau for Saturday and Sunday. We would either be flown over in the five-seat site plane, or we would get onto a forty-foot personnel boat. They had a deal with a hotel in Nassau, where we would get a room really cheap. We would take in some entertainment and buy things we needed. I found out that the locals all went to a shopping center inland on the island. One time, I asked this cab driver to take my wife and me up there, and he acted dumb and told me there was no such place. I told him, "I am from Andros, and if you don't want to take me, I will get a different cab." All of a sudden, he remembered where that was.

On one trip, we went to a nightclub where a James Bond movie segment was filmed. It was fun to go to Ralston Square down by the docks where cruise ships would come in and buy things. They would ask a high price, but I would offer them less. We would get going verbally. We would draw a crowd and sometimes, I would get the lady to agree to the price by the flipping of a coin.

They had a torpedo boat and they had put a deck across the stern so we could go out fishing once in a while. On one trip, my wife caught a big Bull Dolphin. It was good eating. I liked collecting things from the sea. I had a desire to get a big set of shark teeth to bring back to the States. We were trolling on one trip, and I got a fish, like a small tuna. As I was reeling it in, a big shark took a bite out of it. It went limp in the water, so I reeled it in and put it on the deck. I looked down into the water and there was a lot of blood that had come out of my fish, and there were several sharks circling around. All of a sudden, a huge shark came thru the middle of them. I grabbed my fish, which was still on the hook, and threw it overboard. The shark took one pass and bumped it to check it out and circled around and swallowed the fish and went down with it. I was fishing with eighty-pound line and a steel leader. I fought it for almost an hour and got it to the surface. The two deck hands grabbled poles with hooks on them. They shoved one in each of the sides of the head, and pulled it up onto the area where torpedoes were loaded after a test. At that time, the skipper headed to his room to get his pistol and shoot it for me. Before he could get back, the shark thrusted its head and headed back down under the boat. It took me another thirty minutes to get it back up, but it broke the steel leader and got away. Guess what? I had to buy a shark's jaw for the sea shell collection I owned. While I was trying to get that shark, my wife was moving along the side of the deck. She looked into the water and saw a shark bigger than the one I had lost. It scared her to the point that she was grabbing and holding on really tight, afraid of falling into the water.

We were realizing we would be leaving the island soon, so I put my wife on the plane to Nassau, with some money to go buy a hawksbill turtle from a taxidermist shop for us to take home. As the plane door opened up, she had a Bahamian baby in one arm and a turtle in the other. She yelled, "Look what I got in Nassau!"

The baby's mother was startled and grabbed the baby out of her arms. It was common for one mother to take several babies to a doctor in Nassau. She needed help with the babies, and my wife volunteered. She was sorry that she scared that young mother.

My wife completed her days outside the United States, so the wages she earned were tax free. Because of all the business trips I had to take, and the times wasted trying to get that boat, I had to stay on the island for an extra couple of weeks. She went to Texas to stay with her sister. We put all our belongings into wooden crates to ship back to Florida. I kept out the clothes that I would need to live. At the time, we were living on the base since the company that owned the hotel, and many other houses, raised our rent really high, and we had to move into a construction housing trailer on the base. That worked out okay until someone decided it was unsafe for us to live there. Because I was still not considered management, I had to move into the men's barracks. The wife was put into a management/single women's housing building. The man who was in charge of the building didn't put anybody in with her. They were meant to have two people in each unit, but he was a friend from Alaska, so he told me to go to the bed that I was assigned each day to make it look like I had slept there the prior night, but still go ahead and sleep with my wife. The only problem we had was that the ceilings were all suspended, so the girls living behind us could hear my wife and I when we would get a little amorous, which husbands and wives were known to do. We tried to be quiet.

The British officer who was in charge of scheduling the testing of British ships was a fun guy. One night, we had a bomb fire and party at his house to burn an effigy of a guy that the British hated, and they celebrated Guy Fawkes Day every year. He came and got us in his car called "The Thing." We had lots of food and beverages, and everyone circled the big fire pile, and he lit it off and told the story about Guy Fawkes. After the effigy was burned and the fire was pretty much gone, and everyone was tired of eating food and drinking, he decided to drive us home. He decided to take a shortcut to our house, so he drove around to the end of his house. He drove thru some ashes from the fire, and thru bushes to get to our house. It wasn't a fun ride, but *he* was having fun.

About a week after she left, a British ship came to the base to run some tests. I met a few of the sailors off of the boat and got invited to a party on the boat they were going to have. In the storage room near the bow, they circled a large rope around a support post to make it look like the room was carpeted. They set up a table for drinks. They had lots of Scotch that they brought with them. The drink they offered was Scotch and water. The water was the ice when it had melted. They came around and gave everyone a plate of curry and they kept bringing more and more. I finally had to hide my plate. The party was a lot of fun, but we were a little loud. The boat captain came down and told everyone who wanted to keep partying to get *off* the boat.

At this point, a few of us went to downtown Fresh Creek and got on a boat that took us over to the bar across the way. Well, we proceeded to close that place. Now, we had to figure out how we were going to get back to the other side. The ferry boat had stopped running. The key had been taken out of the motor, so we paddled the boat back to the other side. Unfortunately, the site cab which went back and forth to the village had stopped running also. It was about two miles to the base and we weren't feeling any pain. I had put a piece of plywood over the hole that the air conditioner was in at the cottage we had lived in, so we pulled it off and climbed into the cottage that we had been living in at one time. I knew there were beds in there. So, we slept the rest of the night and took the van back to the base for breakfast in the morning. That was a party I would never forget.

Chapter 6

Working in the Space Program

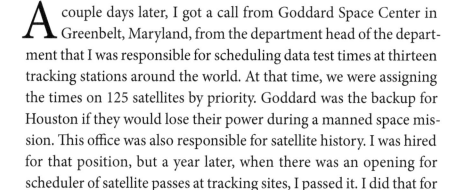

A couple days later, I got a call from Goddard Space Center in Greenbelt, Maryland, from the department head of the department that I was responsible for scheduling data test times at thirteen tracking stations around the world. At that time, we were assigning the times on 125 satellites by priority. Goddard was the backup for Houston if they would lose their power during a manned space mission. This office was also responsible for satellite history. I was hired for that position, but a year later, when there was an opening for scheduler of satellite passes at tracking sites, I passed it. I did that for about four years. It was a great bunch of guys. We worked rotating shifts. Our crew liked to get outside food while on shift. We had a file of all the places that had carry-out menus. Since I was the new guy on the shift, I usually had to make the run.

We had a lot of guys who loved to play basketball, so we ended up putting a team together and joined the Washington D.C. men's league. We got permission to get off one hour before the game, and had to be back one hour after the game. We would then have to make up the time we were gone. I played forward or guard if someone got tired. We won second place, losing by two points. Sometimes, we would play golf after work. A guy on our crew had a friend who owned a bar with pool tables, so sometimes, we would show up at the back door of the bar and the owner would let us in. We would help do a few odd jobs for him. He would give us a couple of beers while we played pool. People asked me, "How can you drink beer and shoot pool at seven o'clock in the morning?"

I would say, "Just like you do at five o'clock in the evenings."

We liked to do things together, so one time, we decided to go fishing and slept overnight at the lake. We had a lot of fun.

My wife and our son David were having a lot of health problems with the high humidity in the Maryland area where we were living. I took my wife and son to a doctor to see what could be done. He suggested trying a dry climate like Arizona. My wife's sister and family lived in Tempe at the time, so I put them on an airplane. In a few days, they both were dried up and breathing well. At that time, we decided we needed to move out there. We sold the house and I quit my job with RCA that I'd held almost ten years. I wished I had stayed long enough to get ten years and a retirement check when I got older.

Chapter 7

Moving to Arizona for health reasons

W e rented a box truck, loaded the car, and away we went. I had our daughter Laura with me, who was still in diapers. As we were going through Oklahoma, my wife saw some flowers at an exit and pulled off to get some. She figured she could catch up with me. I had to stop and get some gas for the truck and she went right past the exit where I had stopped. After about an hour on the road again, I stopped, called the state patrol, told them we had gotten separated, and asked them to look out for her. About 6:00 p.m., I looked for a room for the night, and to feed my daughter. As I was checking out, the credit card I was using was refused because it was outdated. I had a new card, but it was in the car with Ruth. A retired doctor and wife heard what my problem was and paid for the room for the night. I mailed them the money when we got to Arizona.

I checked with the state patrol a couple more times before going to sleep. The next morning, I got a call that she had been located. She was ninety miles ahead of us, at a motel. I jumped into the truck and finally caught up with her. I wasn't a happy person, so I asked her to stay right behind me the rest of the way.

We made a nice profit on the sale of the house, so we were able to find a nice house on the edge of Glendale to buy, with a large backyard for the kids to play in. We wanted to have the kids go to a Lutheran school, and so we found one and joined it.

Living in the Phoenix, Arizona, area in the mid-70s, my wife and I – along with our two children — attended a Lutheran church that also had a school. We thought about enrolling our children in the school when they got old enough. The principal approached me about driving one of the two buses for them, and in turn, not to charge us any fees to attend the school.

They taught me how to drive the bus and paid for my license. The bus was an old conventional Ford that they had bought from the Phoenix school district.

My route was all of the area from Central Avenue to 83rd Avenue. I picked up about thirty students. I drove for two years, until we bought a different house a long way from the school, so we had to enroll our kids into public school and changed Lutheran churches. We sold that house and bought a bigger house, with enough land to have some animals. We had some chickens and turkeys. I wanted to raise some beef, so we went to a cattle auction barn. We walked around, looking at baby calves, and I picked out the two I wanted. The sale started and I got the two I wanted. All of a sudden, my wife wanted to buy this little Guernsey calf. I looked at her and told her with my fingers that we had two, and I didn't want three. The auctioneer thought I was bidding on the calf and announced that the calf had sold for three dollars to the man in the blue hat. I looked around and I was the only one with a blue hat. The calf didn't live for twenty-four hours since it had the scours really bad. The kids enjoyed having the cows, and they knew we were going to eat them. We took both of them at the same time to be butchered. The kids came home on the bus. They ran to the freezer to see the beef, but it was still at the butcher. When we finally got the meat home, the kids would argue which one they were eating at dinner. The packages weren't marked.

I spent lots of time at the feed store getting feed and supplies. They were neat people. One day, I said to them that I would love to have a feed store. They told me that a guy who had a store in Avondale had retired and closed the store down a few months ago. I decided to go out and visit him. Yes, I leased the building. I found a realtor in Avondale, and told her that I wanted to buy a house in the area where I could have animals.

I looked at the house about ten miles west of the store and signed papers. To seal the deal, I drove the forty miles back to where we were living and went to the job where my wife was working. She signed the papers, and I headed back to Avondale. Her fellow workers couldn't believe she signed for a house without checking it out herself. After work, I took her out to see her new house, and she loved it.

The type of bus that I drove

Chapter 8

Hello Missouri

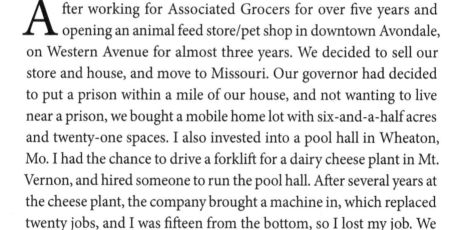

After working for Associated Grocers for over five years and opening an animal feed store/pet shop in downtown Avondale, on Western Avenue for almost three years. We decided to sell our store and house, and move to Missouri. Our governor had decided to put a prison within a mile of our house, and not wanting to live near a prison, we bought a mobile home lot with six-and-a-half acres and twenty-one spaces. I also invested into a pool hall in Wheaton, Mo. I had the chance to drive a forklift for a dairy cheese plant in Mt. Vernon, and hired someone to run the pool hall. After several years at the cheese plant, the company brought a machine in, which replaced twenty jobs, and I was fifteen from the bottom, so I lost my job. We made 58,000 lbs of cheddar cheese per day. I drove the forklift in the warehouse cooler room. It was made and put into 800 lb stainless steel hoops, then stored in the cooler for so many days before it was put into plastic bags inside a big box.

I started working for a man who had a small construction company after I lost my job at the cheese plant. Now I was building barns, etc. Work got slow and he moved to Perryton, Texas, and went to work in the oil fields. I had started a couple of years before that, making plaster craft whiteware to sell to craft shops. I got up to 2,000 molds, plaques, and animals molds, etc. with five employees, from September to December, and then the Reagan slow down started; lots of shops closed doors, and sales dropped really bad.

My aunt offered to pay all expenses if I took her from Springfield, Missouri, to Phoenix, to visit relatives. She said I could sell a pickup load of products that I made up. I sold everything and took orders for another trip.

After I delivered the second load to Phoenix, I decided to stop and visit my old employer/friend in Perryton, Texas. I rode around in the oil fields with him for a couple of days. They wanted to treat me to dinner before I left, and with no air conditioning, I chose to drive at night. I made it one hour away and the engine blew up, so my friend came and took me back to Perryton. He lent me a car to go get my clothes since he had gotten me a job repairing oil wells.

We only repaired oil wells that stopped producing. Sometimes, the pump at the bottom of the well would wear out and we would put a new one in. Sometimes, that could be a real challenge if the old well pump wouldn't release from the bottom when we turned the rods that it was connected to. One time, we finally got all the well oil pipe pulled out, and started putting it back into the well casing, which was a two-man job, and I could get into a rhythm. We were putting the sixty-fifth pipe back into the well casing, when all of a sudden everything came to a stop and the whole workover rig started to shake really hard. We bailed off of the rig and ran out past the safe zone.

It took us two hours to pull out the sixty-five joints of pipe so we could run a chunk of soft lead down into the well and find out what had happened. The well-casing had rusted and collapsed into the well-casing. We put on a grinding stone, which was lowered to the damaged area, and ground thru the damage. After getting it ground up, we put a plug about ten feet below the hole. We poured concrete into the well-casing, until it was about ten feet above the hole. The next day, we drilled through the concrete and finished putting all the pipe back into the well with the new pump. This one-day job ended up being a week-long job.

For the next job we went to, we were asked to remove the pump out of the well, and remove three joints of well pipe since this well wanted to push the oil up with the gas that was also in the well. Everything seemed to go well and we got the pump and pump rods all out with no problems.

We started to remove the well pipe, and the second pipe we hooked onto, and started pulling it out, then we heard a loud oil movement coming up the pipe. In about one minute, it was shooting 105 feet into the air. We had no way to stop it since the well-casing had no valve on it at that time. So, every time the oil stopped shooting up in the air, we would start putting parts on the casing, so we could screw a valve on and shut it off.

After an hour, we finally had it sealed in, with lots of oil on us and on the ground around the work rig. When going on big jobs like this, we always took a sixteen-foot trailer for us to change clothes and eat. I had such a slimy coat of oil all over me, that while walking to the trailer, my pants and underpants started sliding down my legs. As I got to the trailer, both items were down to my ankles. The crew boss overseeing the job sneaked up behind me and sprayed my butt cheek with some window cleaner, and he said, "Yes, there is *some* white skin on you."

Being over forty years old and working in the oil fields was tough, but I got into the swing of things. Most jobs were easy repairs and I had to thank the people who did this, so we could have gas for our cars and other uses.

Please buy me

Perryton, Texas, is a nice little oil town, but if you wanted to go shopping, you would either go up into Liberal, Kansas or south to Pampa, Texas. While on a shopping trip to Pampa, the local National Guard unit was trying to find new people for their unit. I had finished my six-year obligation, but when I started thinking about getting a military retirement, with money and benefits, I decided to sign back up. I wouldn't have to go on active duty, merely start going to monthly meetings and a two-week summer camp. Our son was with me, and he joined, then went to basic training between his junior and senior school years. He attended trade school after he graduated.

I was assigned to the mess section, doing paperwork, since that was the classification I was trained in. Two of the cooks worked for a beer distribution company, so they saved up all the dented cans for summer camp. We started out with twenty-two cases of beer. The company commander and first sergeant would stop by for a cold beer twice a day, and we would take a beer break with them. The food was delivered daily so one of our ice boxes had iced beer in it all the time. We ran out of beer with a few days left in the field, so we chipped in the money, and they put me on the garbage truck. I was dropped off at the commissary. I bought as much as money would allow me, and the truck picked me back up and took me back to camp. I learned that cooks are issued weapons like everybody else. We would wrap them in plastic bags and tape them. At the end of camp, we would take them out of the bags. We would wipe them down and turn them in, unless we fired them.

I drove this type of bus many years

Since the plaster craft business was dead, I had my wife put our trailer park up for sale, and arrange for our trailer to be moved to Perryton. I later took my delivery truck and trailer to Mt. Vernon, Missouri, moving all my plaster craft molds to Perryton. Since it wasn't feasible to open that business back up, I gave all the molds to the Boy Scouts of America in Perryton. I took my old bread truck van, with a trailer behind it, to get the molds. It was going to be a chancy trip, since the license on the truck had recently expired, but the trailer license was current. On the way up there, I got tired and rented a motel for the night.

The next morning, I got back onto the toll road toward Joplin, Missouri, and headed up the highway. I came upon a state patrolman with a car stopped, so I moved over to the inside lane, hoping he wouldn't see the license on the truck. About four miles up the road, the trooper came up on me, with red lights on. I pulled over, stopped, and got out, walking back to his car, and as I got to the back of the truck, I noticed that my trailer was missing. My heart dropped to my feet, and I wondered if it had come off and caused a wreck with some vehicle, or if was in the ditch somewhere.

The officer asked me if I was missing a trailer. He could tell that it was a "yes" by the expression on my face. I told him yes, and he told me it had popped off the ball right after leaving the toll booth and going through a bad dip in the road. He said to follow him to a turn-around spot, then come with him. He said he had to stop and pick up another officer whose car was being worked on, which we did. We got off at the exit where my trailer was sitting up in a car dealer's parking lot near its garage area. We pulled up there; I backed up to the trailer and the mechanic came out. At that time, we had two troopers, myself, and a mechanic looking at the cause, which was wear-and-tear. So, I had to have a new tongue put on it. After the officers left, the mechanic said to me, "Do you realize your plates are expired?" We both laughed that the officer didn't give me ticket.

Chapter 9

Moving to Eastern Washington state

A fter a couple years, and with the price of oil dropping down
to fifteen dollars a barrel, one was lucky to get any work, so I
started running the warehouse for a local department store where the
wife worked. They had three stores in a hundred-mile radius. My wife
and her boss weren't getting along, so we took a vacation and went to
Wenatchee, WA. We had friends to stay with while looking for work,
and I was promised a job when this guy was going to retire at the big
store. So, we returned to Texas, quit our jobs, loaded up all our stuff,
and moved to Wenatchee, WA. We looked like "The Beverly Hillbillies"
going down the road with a bread truck and a pickup hooked up to it,
and a pickup truck with the trailer full of bed mattresses sticking up
into the air. I had to wait for the man to retire, so I picked apples for
my friend who owned an orchard to make some money to live off of.

The bad news was that they laid off ten people only seventeen days
before I was meant to start working for them, and they eventually went
out of business. I couldn't find a good paying job in the Wenatchee
area, so I went to Seattle three hours west of Wenatchee and got a job
working in a pizza supply warehouse. I stayed with my mother, who
lived in Port Orchard, Washington, during the week. I would go home

to Wenatchee, Washington on weekends. Each trip, I would haul a load of stuff to my mother's house. We finished the move the day after our son graduated from high school. On my last trip to Port Orchard with a loaded pickup, I hit an elk out in the road. It rolled up over the hood, crystallizing the windshield. I could see through the middle part of the windshield for the rest of the way to work in Seattle. I was going to drive thru Tacoma after work, but decided it was safer to take the auto ferry boat across to the Port Orchard area. As I was loading onto the ferry, a police officer yelled, "That isn't legal!"

As I passed him, I yelled back, "I know it isn't," and just kept driving onto the boat. He didn't come after me. I got to my mother's house and unloaded everything into an outbuilding. I called my insurance company, and the next day they came and had it hauled to a scrapyard and sent me a check.

The last bus I drove for a school

It's fun jumping out the back which I have to do.

These are fun to sweep.

Try finding a switch in the dark

Try finding a switch in the dark.

The captain's chair (Mine)

Chapter 10

The voyage of the Somerville

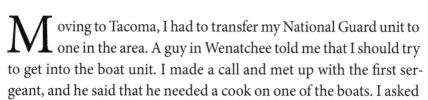

Moving to Tacoma, I had to transfer my National Guard unit to one in the area. A guy in Wenatchee told me that I should try to get into the boat unit. I made a call and met up with the first sergeant, and he said that he needed a cook on one of the boats. I asked him about my son, and they could use him as a marine mechanic. They sent him to school, and so we both ended up in the same unit.

The boat I was put on was from WWII and named the Betsey Ross. The galley was tight so you really had to be friendly. There was not much room for two people to work cooking and preparing meals. The army realized how bad the shape of the boat was in, and ordered us a new boat built in Mississippi. Instead of having it delivered, they asked for our crew to go get it. You had to commit to forty-five days. I couldn't get off of work for that long of a time, but my son was able to do it. When the boat was close to San Diego, they flew the eight of us who couldn't make the full trip to start our two-week summer camp.

Once the boat was tied up, they couldn't get the ramp lowered so customs could get onboard to check the boat. A customs officer had to climb a ladder to get onboard, so he was not a happy guy. He called for help from another officer, who was a neat guy. When the first guy started complaining about the amount of booze in the walk-in storage that crew members had bought cheap along the way, he wanted to confiscate some, since we were only allowed one bottle per person. The other customs officer told him to cool it. All you had to do was give each person on the boat one of the bottles and nobody would lose any. He finally agreed to that. He did find some oranges bought out of the country, and no paperwork to cover them. My son was caught with some bottle rockets in his room, which he was going to shoot off out into the open ocean, but forgot to do it, so they took them.

When the ship came to shore, the head cook was glad to see me. He had a good sense of having a little fun with work. Before the boat left the shipyard to head for Tacoma, he went out and bought some plastic bugs, flies, ants, etc. He liked to decorate the serving area with some of the items now and then. The boat stopped in Port Angeles to pick up the general, who was our head officer in charge over our boat. When cake was served, the general got a piece with plastic flies on it. He got a lot of laughs, took it up to the ship's office, and put it on the skipper's desk with a note asking, "Is this the kind of food you serve on this boat?" He was given another piece, minus flies. The skipper got a lot of laughs out of this, and he still had it in a file cabinet drawer when he retired.

We got a hanging fly strip, which we hung in the officers' dining area. One time, we decorated the big pan of mashed potatoes with green parsley. The football field had a goal post on each end. We had bleachers, with bugs watching the ants playing a football game. This boat had an eighty-foot ramp on the front of the boat, to load vehicles and tanks on and off the shore. For our first summer camp, we took the vessel up the Columbia River to the tri-city area. We were the largest vessel to make it to where we loaded twenty-eight tracked vehicles to take to Ft. Lewis. There, they brought out a floating crane barge and tied it to us. They then brought out little landing vessels that had a ramp in the front. The crane would set a tracked vehicle onto the boat, and they would land it on the beach at Ft. Lewis like it was war time.

Our general from headquarters wanted us to land our boat on the shore with our long ramp, and drive the track vehicle off the boat. It went smooth until it was time to lift the ramp up and back off the beach. The bad news was that it was the day of the year with the lowest tide in the afternoon and we were stuck on the beach. We tried to be pulled off the beach by an army tug, but we had to wait for the tide to come in and float the boat. We were supposed to be back to our pier at 3:00 p.m., but we had to feed everyone, so we took up a collection and they brought down a jeep to pick me up and take me to a grocery store. The head cook had left the boat since he was scheduled to go on vacation, so a jeep took him to meet up with his wife. We didn't get back to our pier and tied up until about 9:00 p.m.

During the year, we would do little weekend runs around Puget Sound for training. Once a year, we would go out to the ocean and fire our fifty caliber guns, of which we had two. I was one of the assigned gunners on the boat, but everybody got to shoot them. The first time we shot at a fourteen-foot aluminum boat with floatation stuffed under the seats, so it wouldn't sink. When we got done, it had a lot of holes in it. We thought about taking it to the store where it was bought and asking for a new one. The other fifty caliber gunner and I were sent one weekend to Ft. Lewis's heavy duty firing range for more training. There, we were shooting at old tanks and trucks. We were trained into locking the gun into a position of fire. The next time we went to the ocean, we put a few fifty-gallon barrels in the water to sink.

The next summer, we were asked to transport all of Idaho's National Guard rolling equipment to Anchorage, Alaska, to be used in their annual training and then brough back to Tacoma. The trip up there was a nice trip. Some of the crew were required to stay up there with the boat since the tide changes up and down a lot each day. The head cook stayed, and people to run the power on the boat, plus deck hands. When they weren't working, they could go fishing in a river that dumped into the ocean near where the boat was tied up. They caught some nice salmon, which they froze and took home.

After unloading all the equipment, we were taken to the airport for our plane back to Seattle. We had to kill a few hours waiting for the plane so people found places to sleep. I found a couch that another guy and I laid out on and went to sleep. The guy on the couch was accused of snoring really loud, but when he got up and walked away, they realized it was me. The head cook was my roommate and kept telling everyone that I was a really loud sleeper. Nobody believed him, but they became believers. He would wear earplugs when he went to bed, so he could get some sleep.

We fixed our room up with mirrors and carpeting. During camp, we would bring a bottle of alcohol, which we would put above the ceiling so nobody would find it. After we closed down the galley for the night, we would grab a couple of sodas, and a big glass of ice, and take it to our room so we could have a drink and play Cribbage. When we were out of soda, we would go to sleep. Being a cook, you worked long hours. When you got into rough weather and big waves, you had to adjust the way you cooked. There were racks on the stove you pulled up to keep the pots on the stove. Tied to the stove at the grill area was a rope which had a large knotted ball on one end which we would tuck under our armpit so we wouldn't fall back while using the grill. Making an omelet was a real chore, and trying to keep the eggs in a small circle was fun to do.

When we were in bad weather, we would have to take bedsheets, get them damp, and put them on the tables. By doing that the metal serving trays that food was served on wouldn't slide back and forth on the Formica-covered tables. There were straps on the bottom of the chairs, so one could keep the chairs from sliding if they were screwed into the floor. One time, I came into the dining area, and the head nurse was sliding back and forth past her tray of food. She didn't secure her chair, so I grabbed a chair and held her in one spot, so she could finish her meal.

While on a long trip, we would find things to do when not on duty. We collected some money and bought a really nice big dartboard, which we mounted on a wall in the dining area. We would have dart competitions on long trips. On the trip to Alaska, my son and I won first place. My son was really good at throwing darts. Sometimes, when we were tied up, he and I would find someplace that had dartboards and play.

The boat skipper loved to fish, so at least once, we would stop and fish for about four hours. The back ramp would be lowered down and they would put the metal lifeboat in the water for a couple people to fish out of. They would tie it to the boat so they didn't drift away. We always would stop in Ketchikan to get fresh produce and milk. The head cook would give them an order on our stop going north, and they would have it ready when we got back to town, and would deliver it to the boat. While there, everyone who wanted to fish would get a one-day license. On one trip, we got into so many fish that we had a hard time cleaning and cooking all of them. On that trip, I picked a couple flats of red cherries at my friend's orchard and carried them onto the plane. Everybody loved them and I was a hero, but we had to cut back putting them out to eat as it was causing too many trips to the toilet for some guys.

We moved into managing apartments in Tacoma while my wife was going to massage school. I was still working in Seattle until the owner fired me one week before he would have had to pay me the last half of the money that I paid an employment company. He agreed to give me half at the end of the first year, and the other at the end of the second. I knew he had done that to save money so I filed a small claims order against him. I had the court papers delivered by a uniformed officer in the morning when all employees would be there. My friend Gary told me that the owner was not happy I did that. He sent a certified check the day before the court day. He wrote stuff on the back of the check, like "I admitted to being a bad employee and I would stop all court orders against him." It was funny, but in the two years working for him, he gave me two pay raises.

Chapter 11

Driving school bus

My wife got a State of Washington grant to go to a massage school funded by the state, and at the end, she was given a license. At the same time, I got a call from Wenatchee to see if I would like to be the warehouseman for a small fire sprinkler company, which I did, but the company — which was based in Renton, Washington — closed the Wenatchee office down a year after I was moved up to manager of that office. The man who was running the office tried to force the owner to rent him an office downtown. The owner asked me if I could build him an office in the warehouse, which I ended up doing, not knowing that it was going to be my office. The old office manager got mad at the owner, and one day, when I came back from Moses Lake where we were doing a huge job, I looked around the office and things didn't look right. After a walk around, I saw his personal stuff was gone, and so I checked the file cabinet, and all the contracts for upcoming jobs were gone. I called the owner in Seattle and told him what had happened. He said he suspected that he might do something like that. He asked me to contact all contractors in the area who used the company and told them what he had done. He never got another sprinkler job in the

Wenatchee area, until he died of a heart attack. I completed the big job in Moses Lake and then a fruit warehouse expansion.

As the new manager, I located a company who said they could put all the underground pipes thru the parking lot and into the sprinkler valve house with a four-foot high, eight-inch riser pipe in the middle of the room. All went well until we put a pressure tester on the top of that, and it was supposed to hold 200 pounds of pressure. Well, he didn't pour any concrete around the ninety-degree fitting, so with all the pressure, that piece of pipe blew apart and was like a missile coming out of the ground. We then had to put it in correctly. I was pushing the carpenters to hurry up and finish the rooms that apples were stored in so I could get my sprinkle pipes in and be the first subcontractor done on the job, and a feather in my hat. The bad news was that we got all the pipe in, and when we filled the pipes to do a pressure test for leaks, it looked bad since all the four and six-inch pipes had to be replaced because the welds on these pipes were leaking. It was a semi-trailer and a half that had to be pulled off the job and be replaced, at the expense of the pipe supplier. Guess what? I ended up being the last contractor off the job.

That ended up being my biggest job, while being the boss before he closed down. The company was having problems with employees in the Seattle area ripping him off so he closed everything down, including my office. The sad thing was that I was making him money.

I then found a job engraving and installing head stones for local cemeteries which didn't last long as the owner was hard to work for. I saw an ad for a groundskeeper for a tennis club which I took but after a year I was laid off due to money issues of the club. I enjoyed the job, mowing all the lawns and trimming shrubs. I would go up after dark once a week and replace outside light bulbs. When it snowed, I would get out the snow blower and shovel out and clear the walks.

One winter we had so much snow we ran out of places to put the snow. We rented a dump truck and front loader to clear off the snow.

After work, I would stop at the Elks lodge for a refreshment and had become good friends with the owner of one of the best real estate companies in town, who managed over 400 rentals for property owners. I told him what had happened. He told me to get a contractor's license, get bonded and insured, and said he would give me all the work I wanted as a contractor to his company, which he did, and I formed Stedman Home Repair.

Now that I had a company, I was looking at the future for my wife and me. I found a healthcare company and decided I needed to look at some kind of retirement plan since I wasn't getting any younger.

Chapter 11

Driving school bus

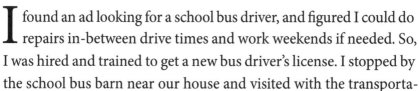

I found an ad looking for a school bus driver, and figured I could do repairs in-between drive times and work weekends if needed. So, I was hired and trained to get a new bus driver's license. I stopped by the school bus barn near our house and visited with the transportation boss about driving bus for them. He told me that I would have to be a substitute driver to start with since he didn't have any openings at the time. He took me out a few times to refresh my driving skills and to learn Washington State driving rules for bus drivers.

He scheduled a time for me to get tested at the motor vehicle testing office. I drove over there and met up with the tester that everyone called "Officer Smiley," since he never smiled for anybody. I had passed the written test the day before and I passed the driving test with ease. He had me drive to a parking lot behind a shopping mall where he had me back the bus up between parking lines and go through the using of all the equipment that a driver uses. We walked around the outside of the bus as I was explaining to him all the parts and their function. We headed up the highway for a few miles and then returned to the testing office. Guess what? I passed with flying colors, but he never smiled at me the whole time so his nickname was true.

In those days, no one had cell phones, but most business people like me carried a pager so when they needed to get hold of me, they would page me and I would find a phone and return the call.

Because of having a pager, they could get hold of me quickly. I got the most call ins for substitute driving hours between doing home repairs. I did several home repairs on the boss's house so maybe that had something to do with getting all the calls. Some times they would have me meet the bus on its route which was being driven by the mechanic. I would take over driving the bus and he would take my truck back to the bus barn.

The only way to get on driving a daily route was for someone to retire, die or get physically ill and have to quit driving. If a bus was getting overloaded, they would have to add another bus which I saw happen many times with all the new houses being built in the area.

Because of a new development of homes being built, I got hired full-time and then that development required three buses. Each bus made a trip picking up high school and junior high, and delivered them to school, and returned to pickup grade school kids. They also had separate buses picking up pre-school and handicapped students. The first route required me to stop at one grade school and pick up a few kids and go one mile to another school for the rest of the students.

The first day, one of the students I had picked up at the first school didn't get off at the one stop I had before I picked up at the second school. After loading the rest of my kids, I headed up the hill to the development I was hired to drive to. I got a call on the radio asking if this student was still on my bus. Since this was my first day on the job, I didn't know the kids, so I asked the other students if she was on the bus, since I figured they would know each other. So, I called in to dispatch and said she wasn't on the bus so they attempted to check with the other bus to no avail. I returned to the bus garage when I was empty. After parking the bus in its parking spot, I started pumping the air out of the brake system and next thing a little girl's head popped up above the seats. The missing kindergarten girl had slept the whole trip and nobody bothered to tell me. A happy mother came to the bus garage and picked her up. She never did that again, but several times over the years, I had it happen again. That was why drivers were required to walk to the back of the bus at the end of the day to make sure there are no sleepers on board. They now had put on buses an alarm switch on the back wall which the driver must go to the back and turn it off after shutting down the motor.

Most people were not aware of the rigid training required now to get a C.D.L. (Commercial Driver's License) as you need to know all the working parts of a bus and the state rules pertaining to driving a school bus before you get behind the wheel and actually drive it. Once one finally got trained and passed one's written and driving test, one would get a Class B (CDL) which allowed you to also drive bobtail delivery trucks and small dump trucks that required a class B license.

Having a class B license and driving for a company or school district subjected employees to a random urine test for drugs or breath test for alcohol. You *must* take the test when asked. Usually, it was done in groups and employees got into a school van and went to a clinic. As a group, we'd all have to stay there until all had passed. Sometimes, it could be a long time if someone has to drink a bunch of water to pass the test. Once, we had to wait for forty-five minutes. They usually did it in the morning which messed up one's plans for the morning. They would call your bus and tell you to come straight to the office after parking your bus. You knew then what that was.

Most small rural districts hired a company to come to their facility in a small bus or with a trailer, or they would use one of the bathrooms.

If you were involved in an accident with your bus, and whether you were at fault or not, you still had to be tested, which protected the school district. At an approach to the road coming out of a housing development, the road tilted to the right and my bus slid into the ditch. Another bus came out and got my students and took them to school. They had to close down the road since the ice and snow were all over the road. The wrecker was having troubles pulling me out so they had to close the road so he could be in the middle of the road and pull me out of the ditch. Yes, I got to go to town and take a urine test. If on your own time you get a D.U.I., you automatically lose your class B license for several years before you can get it back if you fail it.

The thing that really upset school bus drivers was that we had to spend hundreds of dollars to get our license, yet John Doe, who as an accountant or something like that for forty years, could go down and buy a forty-foot motor home, hook up a boat or car behind it, and head down the road with no experience driving something that big and towing something down the road. What would upset us was that they didn't have to get any special training or license; and all they did was get in our way. Over the years I have backed people's boats down a boat ramp at a lake as they were holding everybody up from getting on the lake and catching some fish. Not everybody could back trailers up.

With twenty-five years of bus driving, I got to meet lots of interesting people, with all kinds of backgrounds and personalities. Most people who drove bus loved children, and the ones who started driving with the attitude that it was merely a job usually got hooked on it because of the fun with kids. I got attached to most of the kids and I was special to them. I had a few who tested me, and I had to be stern with them.

One got attached to them more when one got to know them more. I had a boy at my last stop who would put a piece of chocolate candy on my knee every morning, and said, "Good morning, Mr. Bus Driver." He had a froggy voice. On one route I had, I would reverse the order of dropping the kids at home on Friday afternoons. The students who got on early on the route would be later getting home. The parents and kids all loved it. I would get approached in a store or they would come up to my wife and me while we would be out having dinner, and they'd let me know how much they loved me. While up in East Wenatchee, Washington, eating dinner, a waitress came over to our table and asked me what my name was. She said, "You were my bus driver in school."

I thought I knew who she was, but couldn't remember her name so I asked her if she had lived up on a hill with a long driveway, and a brother who kept talking about putting his head in the mailbox. She said, "Yes," and was so happy to see me. I still have students who I am in contact with that say I was their favorite driver.

Over the years, I had a small home repair business, and I would ask some of the older boys if they wanted to make money and help me. Some stayed with me after they graduated until they found a full-time job. I was invited to more than one graduation and the party afterwards, which I considered an honor. I must have been liked well-enough since they never threw eggs on my house or spray-painted anything I owned.

After over fifteen years of driving at this medium-sized school district and working for several transportation supervisors, I found some had a good sense of humor. One time, the boss and another driver pulled every bus out of the garage, and the backed them into different locations, and another time, the keys to all the buses were put into a bucket so you had to dig around until you could find your keys since they weren't marked very well, which made a good

April Fools' joke. We found out who did that; he was a retired state patrolman who drove many years. He had a great sense of humor, but we wanted to kill him that morning. Most of them were good, but some were hard to work for, so I retired the first time, and decided to substitute for other school districts in the area. Part of that time before I retired, I was the shop steward and secretary for the union at that district, working with the superintendent and being involved in contract renewals. One time, the superintendent grouped several items we were trying to get changed; we agreed with him and he grabbed all his papers and started to leave the room. I said, "Excuse me, but what about the last three items we haven't talked about." He turned around and slammed his papers on the table and sat down. He wanted to get out of there so he agreed to all of them.

The first type of bus I drove in Washington

Cross bar so kids have to walk around.

Every year, on the first day of school, I always wore my baseball hat with a pony tail on the back so the kids would think I was some kind of hippie guy. I would tell them my name and that my nickname was "Bear," and if they treated me nice and took care of my bus and kept it clean, I would treat them well, but if not, I would turn into a bear. I would start out as a little koala bear or I could become a *grizzly* bear when you would lose your privilege to ride the bus. I would tell them that they would get treated with treats once a month for keeping the bus clean. I usually treated them with candy. I gave them to the students when they got off the bus; that way, if they choked while eating it, they wouldn't be on the bus and throw the paper on the floor. After telling them everything, I would take my hat off and wipe the sweat off my forehead, then watch them laugh because I had tricked them. I became a father figure or grandpa to some of the kids whose home life wasn't good.

I had to become the mean bus driver at times, and I had, over the years, written up students who sometimes would lose their bus privilege for a period of time. Each year, students who had earned the honor of a seat assigned up front by me (because they had caused problems in the back) would start the new school year being allowed to return to the back. One boy kept getting moved to the front next to me. When school started on the third year of riding with me, he sat up front the first day of school. I told him he could go to the back, and he said, "I like it up here." He rode the whole year up there and we became friends. I had three boys from the same family who got kicked off the bus for causing problems. The father called the transportation boss and wanted to have a meeting with the boss and me since he thought I was the problem. One by one, the boys were called into the boss's office, with the father, my boss, and me. They admitted to teaming up to cause problems on the bus. They agreed to write me "I'm sorry letters," and promised never to do it again, then they became good riders on the bus.

The next to last day of school each year, I would bring a cooler full of popsicles, and would use my grandkids or a student who got off the bus near the end of the route to hand them out as they got off the bus. One year for a change, I gave them a soda and a popsicle while still in the school parking lot. I had to use a spare bus that day since mine was being worked on. I walked through the bus, giving them a soda if they wanted one. I went thru handing out the popsicles, and I went back and forth with a big plastic bag, and collected cans and wrappers when they were done, and when I parked the bus, I found one stick on the floor and no cans or wrappers. Everybody (other drivers) thought I was a fool, but I had the best group of kids as far as I was concerned.

Since I was now semi-retired, I let all the small schools in the area know that I was available if they needed a substitute driver for a day or two. I really didn't want to work every day since I had my home repair money to live off of. One school used me a couple of times. They were a small school, with fifty students at the school up through sixth grade, so they had two buses: one for the young students and the rest were picked up and taken to the junior and senior schools in the town thirty miles away. The school was located back up in a coulee. The road had hills on both sides of it. The U.S. Air Force would send jets down it at low levels and scare the hell out of you. Then, they would turn left and go down the Columbia River.

After seventeen years at the big school, I decided to retire due to new rules. My construction repair job was keeping me too busy and I wanted to work only now and then, so I substituted at some small schools.

I got called to a small school fifteen miles north of where I lived to fill in for the driver with the biggest route, so he could watch his daughter pitch softball for the high school team at some home games. I did this several times since I knew him quite well and worked for his dad, who owned a big orchard in my junior and senior school years. This driver also had a small orchard in the town of Orono.

About ten days before school was meant to start for the new year, I got a cell phone call from the transportation boss, asking if I had heard what had happened to the driver I had substituted for. I was out on a lake in my boat fishing for Sockeye salmon, and all of a sudden, I had a fish on, so I told him I would call him back and hung up. The sad thing was, I lost the fish while messing with the phone, but I did get my limit.

I called him back and he told me the driver had been in a wreck with his motorcycle and was banged up pretty bad. He asked if I would cover for him for two or three months, since I wasn't working anywhere. I told him yes and started the year on the longest route of the three buses they had. I would pick up the first student at 5:50 a.m., and go up the Columbia River, driving into orchard complexes and other housing developments to where the Chelan school district stopped, picking up students. When I got back to the school with the students, I would meet a bus from Waterville which the students had a choice which high school or jr. high school they wanted to go to. I would then take the other students to the schools twenty miles south where they went since the main school was for young students only. This route was 105 miles per day, and they had their own fuel tank at the school and garage to keep the buses in.

Instead of driving the bus back twenty miles and returning to the school in the afternoon, they had a school car there for me to drive back and forth. It was a great benefit since they paid the fuel. I kept the car at home and when it was nasty, it got parked in the garage so I didn't have to scrape ice off the windows. I also drove to field trips and a few sports trips, like volleyball and track. They were fun to take on sports and field trips. After the games were over or heading home from a field trip, we always stopped for food. I let them pick the place with the coach's approval. This was a treat for most of them, and bus drivers and coaches got free meals at burger stops. The kids would be happy on the way home after having some food, and most of the time, they would start singing songs. Most of the time, they would start singing "The "Wheels Go Round and Round." When they got done with their songs, I would get their attention and tell them it was my turn to sing a song, which was "Row, Row, Row Your Boat, underneath the stream. Ha Ha fooled you all, I'm a submarine." I got them into singing that song.

With eighteen years in the military, and active in the American Legion, I volunteered to be their person at the school to arrange a Veterans' Day program.

On two different years, I arranged for old military vehicles to be brought out to the school by some veterans who loved to display their Jeeps and trucks. They would let the kids get into them, ask questions, and take pictures.

The last ten years, I was in an army watercraft unit, with most of the years on a new vessel we got in 1988. Our crew went to Mississippi and picked it up at the shipyard where it was made. I couldn't get off for forty-five days, but flew to San Diego, California and helped bring it the last part of the mission, which qualified me as a "Plank Owner" on the vessel, which was the first crew to operate the vessel. I was second cook the whole time on the vessel. The vessel's name was the General Somerveil, and it had been moved to Hawaii permanently. We did one Veteran's Day on the U.S. Army and its different types of boats and showed pictures of my ship. Most people were not aware that the army had more boats than the navy. The navy had ships, and the army had boats. They had a lot of tug boats of different sizes and landing vessels of different sizes. The army had ships.

The last Veteran's Day program, I purchased an M.R.E. (Meal Ready to Eat) from a store in Wenatchee which carried military supplies. I asked one of the older boys to help me start the program. I had brought two small fry pans, and he and I hid in a room outside the gym where the program was going to be. After everyone was in there, the teacher had us come in. I told him to hit the pans together since I had one and he had another. He got carried away and was swinging his pan at me. It was quite an entrance and I told the kids that cooks were trained in pan-to-pan ware fare. That got a lot of laughs from everyone. I also brought a ten-gallon army cooking pot so kids could see how big of pots we used sometimes when feeding a lot of people, and not giving them M.R.E's while out in the field. I opened the box, and explained and showed the students what most soldiers out fighting in the war zones eat.

This little school wanted to make sure I kept driving for them, so during the summer, they asked me to do some painting in my spare time. I ended up painting the inside of thirteen classrooms, the out-side of the administration building, and the outside of the bus garage during the summers I was there.

At times, they had trouble getting people to drive bus due to the weather, since it got very hot, and had no air conditioners on the busses, and the winters could be hard since some years there was lots of snow and ice. They finally got smart and bought buses that had drop chains, which were pieces of chains on a shaft inside the duel on both back wheels. With the flip of a switch, these chains dropped down, and the inside tires drove over the chain as it rotated under the tires. These saved one from having to manually install metal chains on the bus. But they weren't good on ice. Over the years, I put lots of chains on busses.

One year, the bus with the young students on it was headed south, back to the school early in the morning and a box truck out of Yakima came around the corner, heading north, and the driver fell asleep and crashed into the front of the bus at the right-hand corner. The driver steered it so it wouldn't be a head-on collision. There is a fruit-packing business/orchard right next to where the accident happened. A lot of the parents of the children on the bus worked there and the noise was so loud that the employees came running out to help the injured children, and smooth the emotions of their own kids on the bus. The truck also hit a car driven by a girl who used to go to school in Orondo. The driver got hurt, but her sister was killed. If she wouldn't have been in the car with her sister, she would have been on the bus.

The driver immediately called the office after the police and two buses were sent to the scene, and the children were divided between the two buses, and were used as ambulances by the state trooper, with parents riding on the buses trying to sooth the kids until they got to the hospital that was twenty-five miles away. The hospital had all available doctors and nurses at the emergency entrance to receive the buses with a police escort. The children all recovered, but the driver still had problems from it.

A large dairy farmer from up north of the school donated 300 pounds of thin sliced beef for a large awards lunch on the playfield to honor the kids involved. The state patrol awarded the driver for her actions of not having a head-on wreck, but taking the wreck on the front door. As an army cook and used to cooking large amounts of food at a time, I volunteered, plus two other men, to cook all the meat and the school cook arranged everything else. A few months later, a truck loaded with fruit didn't notice a bus stopped with left turn signals on, locked up his brakes, and hit the back of the bus, damaging it pretty well, but had no injuries, and he got a big ticket.

In the mornings, when I had to meet the transfer bus from Waterville school district, I would get ahead on time, which would get me to the schools where these kids went too early, so I would stop for about ten minutes at a convenience store along the way, and let the kids go in and get something to eat, as long as garbage went into the trash can up front. Some kids would come out with a big bag full since they would put stuff in their lockers to eat if they didn't like the lunch. In the afternoon, I would meet the bus from Waterville at a convenience store in Orondo. I had to stop letting the kids go in for food since three of them went to the Subway sandwich area and we had to wait a long time, so everyone lost that privilege.

After five years as a substitute driver at the Orondo school, fighting the cold winters and hot summers and falls seasons, my wife and I decided to move back to Arizona and the drier climate. The students gave me a four-foot-long banner, with drawings and goodbye messages on it, plus a glass award thanking me for everything I had done for them. After that many years, I got attached to a lot of them, and I am still in contact with some of them.

The kids loved me and gave me a great farewell.

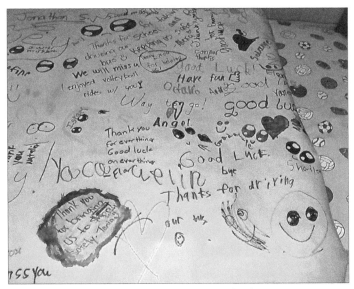

They were a great bunch of kids!

During spring break on the fifth year, my wife and I flew to Arizona to visit an old boss when I was in the fire sprinkler business. I ran his Wenatchee office. I contacted my cousin who lived in Tempe, and asked her if she knew of an honest real estate agent who could help us find a good home to buy. He showed us houses for two days, and on the second day, we signed papers for the house we are now living in.

The fun began since we had five houses to sell and get rid of, along with all the tools and supplies I had collected in twelve years in the house we were living in. You don't realize how much stuff you have collected and brought home after doing a repair job for someone or working on one of your own properties. We had three sales, as well as the veterans retail store checking for things to sell in their store. I still took several trips to the dump.

The day after school was out, I headed for our new home in Arizona in my Ranger pickup, with an eight-foot utility trailer behind it. The bed of the pickup with the shell on it was totally full with shop tools and equipment that I wanted to take to Arizona. The trailer was full of yard things like a BBQ and lawn chairs, etc.

When I arrived at our new house, I put the truck and trailer in the garage, met up with the real estate man again, and started looking for a four-plex rental property to buy so I could re-invest some of the properties profit, plus have a place for our grandson who wanted to move down there with us. I was able to find one seven miles from where we were going to live, so I bought it and returned to Washington state, then finished selling our rentals and planning the move down. I rounded up a crew of friends and relatives to load the twenty-six and fifteen-foot U-Haul trucks I had rented. I drove the big truck and our daughter and her husband drove the small truck, with a trailer behind it and our car on it. It took us two-and-a-half days to get to the new house. My wife and grandson flew down.

After a few months of getting our home set up, sorting out all my tools, setting up a little workshop, and doing a few repairs at the four-plex that needed to be done, I got bored.

While doing some scanning on the computer, I found an ad for bus drivers needed with a small, private bus company. I set up an appointment to talk to them about driving at a small school part-time near Tempe, Arizona for $22.00 per hour.

The next school year, I was the only driver since the other two drivers didn't come back. The bus manager sent me the papers for the two routes. One route ran on Monday and Thursday only. The other route was Tuesday and Friday only. There was no school on Wednesday for anyone. The other third of the students were on computers only with the school. I drove each route in my car and found several problems to the route sheets, which was corrected before school started. I drove two different buses on different days. It was a little confusing at first.

After a couple of months, they merged the two routes into one, so that made a big route, but some students stayed at home. After Christmas break, all students came to school and another driver was hired, with me as the lead driver. I was in charge of getting all the daily report sheets sent to the bus manager's office. I also was in charge of keeping the busses running, and purchasing things that we might need, and reporting any problems so they could be repaired at night, or get another bus to school for the next day.

This was a private school and they only had about 100 students. They had a small, fenced animal area, which had a pot belly pig that the kids could feed. They hatched some chicken and duck eggs, and they fed, watered them, and got to hold them. As the ducks got older, they got a little pond to swim in, and the chickens got a small chicken coup to get out of the weather and have a place to lay eggs. It was great to see the students learning about how to take care of animals since most of the kids lived in apartments and came from families struggling to make it month-to-month, and a lot of them didn't have a father at their home. Sometimes on Fridays, they would get a bag of food to take home. The first time, they gave them the food as they were walking out of the school; some were getting on buses and you could guess what a mess I had when I got back to the school at the end of the run. From then on, they were put into tubs in the front seat of the bus, and they would grab one as they got off. Needless to say, that resolved the messy bus problem. The students' names were above the seat they were assigned, and about ninety percent followed the rule; they became good students to haul.

At Christmas time one year, they set up stations around the outside of the school building for the parents to stop at and get different items for the students and family. They worked with different businesses and vendors to supply things at these stations. They got a sandwich and drink to start off with, and at other stations, they got shoes with their names on the box as they were sized up ahead. Another stop got new winter coats, and so I would see a lot of kids with the same designer coats every day. The last stop was where I was. Playing Santa Claus for a lot of years, I volunteered to be it for the school. I was told that someone had hired a Santa so I wasn't needed, so I instead volunteered to give out candy canes to the students at the last station. Fifteen minutes before the party was meant to start, the principal came up to me and said that Santa wasn't coming. I was afraid this would happen, so I had my suit in the trunk of my car and quickly put it on and saved them. My wife handed out the candy to the students. The last stop was a wrapped gift, with their name on it. They found out what they wanted ahead of time and got volunteers to purchase items for the students within a price range.

This little school was fourteen miles away from our house here in Mesa, Arizona, which meant driving fifty-six miles per day, four days per week in my personal car, and after turning seventy-six years old, I decided it was time to retire permanently, without causing any wrecks with my school bus.

I had a woman at the first school district who had backed out of her driveway, and hit the bus backside panel by the rear wheels, tearing up some metal on the bus. At least, I was heading back to the bus garage empty after having dropped my students off. The police were called and they gave her a ticket, but she insisted it was my fault.

At the time of the wreck, the transportation manager had a man who repaired damage to buses, so he came over and figured out what he needed to repair it. The wreck was on Thursday morning and the bus was ready for me to drive on Monday morning, 100% repaired. On Wednesday morning, the insurance company that represented the lady who caused the wreck showed up at the bus garage, and wanted to see the wrecked bus and take pictures. The transportation manager laughed and told him it was out picking up students, and showed him the pictures he had taken. I guess if you snooze, you lose. I almost had another accident on the other end of this block during the winter, with snow on the ground. I was driving back toward the bus garage, and I noticed an older gentleman bent over a snowblower with his head down, not looking where he was going. So, I stopped the bus and when he stopped and looked up, he was about two feet from running into the entrance door of the bus. You should have seen the expression on his face!

SPORTS AND EXTRA TRIPS

I personally enjoyed doing sports trips and educational trips to other cities. It would give me a break from my regular route, plus a chance to make extra money since some of the trips would take several hours, and sometimes, I would have more than one team and they would have to use the same field or floor. After all the games were done and the kids had changed clothes, I had to take them to eat before driving home most of the time. Sometimes, I wouldn't get home until 2:00 a.m., and I'd be back at the bus garage at 6:00 a.m. to get ready for the morning bus run.

The school district fired one transportation leader because he tried to upgrade the system with a few new buses, and they didn't like him spending the money, so they fired him. They brought in a retired transportation leader from another district where he was hated. I had a couple of run-ins with him. He made a new rule that if one came in after 1:00 a.m., he or she couldn't drive the morning bus run for lack of sleep. The first time it happened to me, I wrote three hours of sick leave on my time-sheet.

When he saw that, he called me into the office, asking what I thought I was doing. I said, "You say I am not fit to drive, so I am taking sick leave pay." He said, "I am going to check this out at the district office." The next day, we had a drivers' meeting and he told everyone I had put in sick leave pay for coming in late, and it was approved, so everyone could do that now.

One day, I was in his office and a box arrived, and he couldn't find anything to cut open the box, so I reached into my pocket, got my pocket knife out, and opened it. He said, "What are you doing with that knife in your pocket? You aren't allowed to have a knife on the bus." So, he went back to the district office, and guess what? I won that one also, as long as it was only a little pocket knife.

A new extra route came open in the mornings so I applied for it, and he said that I wasn't qualified to haul pre-school children, even though for many years, I was hauling kindergarten students at noon every day. I took that problem to the union representative and guess what? He lost again.

He decided to retire again, and so the district put the task of supervising all the drivers on the maintenance boss since both departments worked out of the same building. It worked out most of the time, but I had become the shop steward for the union, representing the drivers and maintenance workers, so we butted heads now and then. He picked on one of the drivers a lot so we got into it now and then. This arrangement didn't last more than a couple of years since they found out he was using transportation money on building projects instead of new buses.

While he was still our bus department leader, we got involved with the Relay for Life cancer walk, which was held every year, and we had two drivers that where cancer patients at one time. One got it again and passed away, while still an active driver. He let us put a team together to walk the track for twenty-four hours. We wanted to make a good donation from our team of drivers and maintenance men, so we did a super big yard sale, which got us a couple thousand dollars. One of the drivers used to make kettle corn for a living and still had the equipment, so we got the supplies we needed. Since the weather was still cold, we backed two buses out of the garage and would make over one hundred bags at a time. The school mail courier would take orders at all the schools he went to, and after we made it, we would load the van full of kettle corn. We would make a lot of money from this project to donate to the American Cancer Society. One year we donated over $8,000.

If you had a team, you had to have a man dress like a woman and collect as much money as you could in a set time frame. The first year, I got chosen to be the person. While on a field trip to Yakima, Washington, with another driver on a Saturday after dropping the kids off on an all-day function she and I headed down town to check out thrift stores to buy a bra, dress and shoes. One of my wife's clients donated a blond wig. I was trying on a dress and an officer from my National Guard unit came into the store and saw me so guess what, I had to do some quick explaining while he was laughing.

The first year, I came in second place and the guy who won first place got a nice fishing pole and tackle box. We only had to wear the dress for two hours. This made me want to win first place the next year. I got the same driver to go looking with me for a sexier dress for the next year which was a black and white striped dress.

The second year we really put a lot of effort in being the top team. We held back some of the money we had made to put in my purse. At the end of the wearing the dress I turned in the money I had collected in the four hours. I walked around the track asking people to give me a donation. I would tell them that for one dollar, I *wouldn't* kiss them. I got lots of laughs and money too. On one lap, while next to our camp, a man told me he would give me $4.00, if I gave this driver who was asleep in a lawn chair a big kiss on the top of his bald head. I told everyone to get their cameras out as I had lots of lip stick (bright red) on. I knew the guy getting the kiss had a great sense of humor, so I proceeded planting a nice, juicy red kiss on the top of his bald head. He came out of the chair really fast and I quickly ran away from him. I told him I was paid to do that, and he saw who paid me and a lot of good laughing followed.

I won first place at midnight after four hours of wearing that dress, and we donated over $8,000. My large red purse did a good job. I was awarded a large hot pizza and a large apple pie at midnight, not the fishing gear the man got last year.

I was chosen to be Mr. Relay!!!

During the year, my wife and I went to Hawaii, and while there, we went to a large flea market. While there, I saw a booth selling dresses and shirts, so I asked her if she had an orange moo moo dress that would fit me. She found one, and I went in the back of her shop and tried it on as she was laughing. I ended up giving it to our daughter after that year's walk. (I came in third), but we all still had lots of laughs. When my brother saw a picture of me in my outfit, he said, "Oh my God, he looks like Mom," It was such a good program and it affected a lot of people. My wife and her friend brought their massage tables there and gave mini massages for money.

While working for the first school in Washington, I personally enjoyed doing sports trips and educational trips to the other cities in our state. It would give you a break from your regular route plus a chance to make extra money.

In the early days, we got paid our regular route money, plus the money on the out-of-town trip, so we had good paychecks if we took the trips. When I was hired, some drivers didn't want to take trips, so I could always get at least two trips per week where I hauled more than one team. Lots of times, it would be two buses. The female driver above me on the seniority board took a lot of trips, and lots of times we would run together. We were asked by students if we were married, and would laugh since she was much younger than me. Unfortunately, we lost the double dip on pay during a union contract renewal to get a pay increase per hour. Some weeks, I would get between forty and sixty hours of pay. As more people moved into the area and the number of drivers increased, more drivers were taking trips. I was then lucky to get a trip each week. Most trips were uneventful, but I will share with you some of my trips that were eventful.

I was scheduled to take the varsity football team to the tri-cities one Friday night in September on a hot day. I took my bus to the fuel station to fuel up, and when checking the engine for the trip, I found it had a fuel leak, so I had to take another bus which was older and was made by Crown bus makers. The bus was sort of round on both ends so they called them "Twinkies," as they looked like one.

This was called a twinkie bus.

On sports trips, they were allowed to eat and drink, so drivers put a few garbage bags throughout the bus. Two brothers, who each ate a chicken sandwich for lunch at the school, both got sick and started throwing up, and nobody could get a garbage bag to them in time, so it ended up on sports bags and on the floor. It smelled so bad that we had to open all the windows on the bus.

When we got to the football field, I found the athletic director for the school and told him what had happened, so he sent a boy to get me a garden hose and sprayer with some disinfectant to make the bus smell good. I positioned the bus so the front door was lower than any other part of the bus, and hung sports bags outside of mirrors so they could be hosed off. I ran the hose through the back window and hosed off the bus floors and seats that needed it. I sprayed off the sports bags outside. I sprayed deodorizer throughout the bus and I got a lot of "Thank you, thank you!" from the coaches and players when they came back from playing and showering.

After eating dinner, we headed home, and about five miles north of Quincy, I blew out a rear tire and had to call a tire company. We had a contract with them to bring us a new tire. The father of the two boys who were sick came and got them, since they still weren't feeling really well. It was after midnight when we got back to the school. That was a trip I wish I hadn't signed up for.

I took a busload of kids from a high school Spanish class to Seattle to see a Mexican band from central Mexico do songs and dances from different part of Mexico. Since it was snowing, I called the Washington state patrol to see if Snoqualmie Pass was open, and I was told no, so we had to take Steven's Pass. To get to Seattle from the Wenatchee area, you had to go over a mountain pass. You can call a phone number to find out road conditions. When both passes were closed, you had to go down to Oregon to get around the mountains. Steven's Pass highway was part two-lane, and had lot of curves, so it was not my choice, plus it doesn't have a big rest stop. About half way to the concert, I started looking for a rest area. Suddenly, on the left side of the road, there was a small county park with about eight portable out houses so I pulled in.

As the students were getting off the bus, the teacher noticed a girl who wasn't in her class. She immediately called the school to see if she was missing from school, which she was told that she was, so she informed them that the girl had hidden on the bus with the help of her friend. They had put her in the corner, with coats covering her, so when the teacher was checking her list, she wasn't noticed. She didn't get to watch the concert and had to sit in the main office of the school. The two girls got into a lot of trouble when we got back to the school.

Sometimes, winter sports trips could get scary and dangerous. I was driving this forty-foot bus loaded with kids, heading to a sporting event, and I was in charge of their safety. We called some of the trips "white knuckle trips" since I had to hold onto that steering wheel and be ready for ice and snow conditions that I had to react to instantly.

One trip, ice and snow started coming down after reaching the tri-city area. We had three buses with lots of basketball players, and the weather kept getting worse. While we were eating, the coaches called the school superintendant with some concern. The options they were looking at were to stay at the school overnight, find motels, or drive home. All three of us bus drivers were veterans and had been driving for lots of years, and the buses we had were some of the newest, so we decided to drive home. The road home was across mostly desert-type roads, with two lanes and very little traffic. We drove the buses in the middle of the road on the crown of the road, and only met a few cars to move over for. When we got to Quincy, Washington, some of the kids needed to go to the bathroom. I pulled into the state rest area and the bus behind me followed me in there. The third bus went by slowly. I pulled out behind it and started down the winding road. At the bottom of the hill, there was a bridge over a canyon. As we know, bridge roads freeze up and get really slick. A Chevy Blazer coming across the bridge got out of control and started doing loops, and the first bus saw it coming toward him and stopped. The car bounced off of the front left bumper before it came to a stop. The state patrol was called and we moved all his students and coaches onto our buses, and finished returning to school, but the other bus driver had to stay at the scene of the wreck.

Near Halloween, I signed up for a volleyball trip to the tri-cities and the head coach owned a mini-mart across the street from my house, so I told her I would be driving on that trip she was scheduled for. A couple days later, she approached me and wanted to know if we could stop at the fruit stand near Quincy where they grew pumpkins, to let the girls each go out into the field and get one. So, she and I collected a lot of big boxes to put them in. We put all the boxes in my storage area. There were two other drivers on this trip, but we didn't tell them what we were doing since this was going to be a secret surprise from the coach and she was paying for them. The coach rode on my bus and I radioed the other buses, and asked them to stay behind per the coach's request, which they did. We got about a mile from the fruit stand and I called the other buses and told them I was having some engine problems, and was going to pull into the fruit stand since it had a large parking lot. When I stopped, the coach stood up and informed the girls that she was buying each of them a pumpkin. She went to the other two buses and did the same thing. As the girls came back with their pumpkins, I wrote their names on them, and placed them in the boxes. That was one of the fun trips I had.

Most of the buses that went to the Yakima area on sports trips would take their players to a fast-food hamburger place called Miners. The coaches liked going there because coaches and drivers got a free meal. When we first started, there was no indoor seating except for the coaches and drivers. We would go through the back door and there were two small tables for us to eat in the kitchen. Everybody else had to sit at picnic tables under a lot of trees around the building. They eventually remodeled, where they could seat over 150 people in the dining area, and had six tables in the kitchen area for drivers and coaches. As you came through the front door and to the left where you ordered, there was a nice big door with a brass sign that read, "No admittance. Coaches and bus drivers only." When you sat down, they would bring over a box with French fries and onion rings in it to eat while we were trying to figure out what we wanted.

One worker would bring out your milkshake, and hold it over your head upside down, and ask if that was thick enough, which made everybody laugh.

One Saturday, I took a girls softball team to Miners and the coaches had never been there before so I had to lead them into the area where the coaches ate. The owner, who was about eighty and a really funny guy, was wandering around the kitchen area; he saw me and came over to our table. I told him the ladies had never been here before. He informed them that they should have been there a few days ago when a guy with a knife stormed in here to rob everybody. He told us that he was over by that door, and the guy turned his back toward him, so the owner pulled out his pocket knife, slit his throat, pulled out his guts, and then walked away laughing. We all had a good laugh at that story. He had a great sense of humor. He married one of his workers about twenty years younger, and the last time I was there ten years ago, she was still running it.

I signed up for a baseball trip one day and when I arrived at the school, this male coach asked me if we were going to stop at Miners on the way home. I let him know we were going to be at least thirty miles east of there. He gave me a sad face. We got to the little town for the game and in the second inning, it started raining really hard and the sky turned black, so the game was canceled for the night. He then approached me about going to Miners. He said, "This was supposed to be a double-hitter and we weren't scheduled to be home until late, so can we go?"

I looked at him and said, "You know how curvy and narrow the road 'Rattle Snake Hill' is, and it would be very dangerous, so maybe we better go thru Yakima, and we will stop and eat at Miners." I told that story to the boss regarding why I drove a lot more miles. His daughter played baseball so he didn't complain.

Several times, the boss asked me if I wanted to go with him out of town to a sporting event that his daughter was playing in. We would take his school service truck. His excuse was that we would have more than one bus there, and he would be available to fix a bus if any of them had any problems. He was a good boss to work for, and unfortunately, cancer got him.

Over the years of driving, I also hauled different kinds of bands, such as jazz or marching bands. I took trips all over the state of Washington and along the Oregon border. The band leader would always bring his wife along on the trips. Most of the band trips were overnight trips. One trip with the jazz band was to the Oregon border, just east of Portland. I arrived at the high school to pick everybody up and the teacher was upset with the bus I was driving. He wanted one of the newer buses for the trip, but I was assigned one of the older Crown (Twinkie) buses. I knew he would be upset so I had checked why we didn't have a newer bus. I was told to tell him if he wanted one of the newer buses, he would have to wait one-and-a-half hours. He wanted to get out of town, so he accepted it. It was two days of competition. The school was about ten miles south of the Washington border, so while they were competing, I drove back across the border, where I was told to fuel up and got some lunch.

After the first day of competition, we drove back to Vancouver, WA, to a motel across the street from a large mall so the kids could shop and find a place to eat. The next morning after breakfast, we returned to the same school as the day before, to complete the competition, in which we won first place. After stopping for some snack foods, we headed up the highway to Tacoma where we stopped for burgers and fries. On the way up Interstate 5, it started to snow. The further north we went, the heavier the flakes got. More than once, I had to pull off the highway and clear the snow off of the windshield, since it got to the point where the wiper area was the only area I could see out of. The side mirrors were pretty covered also. We finally made it to Tacoma safely.

While everyone was eating, I got on the phone and checked pass reports to see which pass would be the safest to go over. The one pass required chains, but Snoqualmie Pass wasn't requiring chains, and it was the better pass, with better roads and a rest area with bathrooms. I told this to the teacher and he agreed with me, so we loaded everybody onto the bus and headed out. When we started up the pass, the highway department changed it to chains required on buses and trucks. I found a safe area to pull off that had been plowed and put the chains on. I had prepared to chain up if I had to so, I had boots, rubber pants and a raincoat with a hood. I had a tarp to kneel on plus gloves, flashlight and an umbrella. I made the teacher hold the light on the wheel hub so I could get the chains over the tires and hooked up. He wasn't really happy about helping but when you travel in the winter you have to be prepared. We drove about twenty miles to get out of the heavy snow and was allowed to remove the chains. We knew we still had another pass that we would probably have to chain up or we could drive an extra forty miles around the end of the mountains so we decided to drive around, which didn't make me mad. We finally made it back to the school with a lot of parents happy that we made it home safely.

A month later, two other buses and I took the high school marching band to Spokane for a night-time light parade, but we left in the morning since it was about four hours of driving time to get there. We had to get everyone into motel rooms. We took up almost the whole motel. I sat on the edge of my bed and ended up on the floor. The mattress was broken, and when I reported it, they didn't have another room or mattress, so I had to live with it.

We took the kids in the buses down the parade route so they knew where they were going and showed everyone where we would be parking the buses. An hour before the parade, we took all the band members to the starting area of the parade and moved our buses where we had told everyone we would be parked. The drivers went to a place to have dinner since we knew they wouldn't be at the buses for at least three hours.

The next morning after we got everyone fed, we went to a mall for some shopping and lunch before heading home. On the way home, the lead bus hit a large elk and broke the headlight holder on the right side. The elk ran into the woods. I looked at the problem, went to my bus, and got a roll of white one-inch medical tape out, and taped the light back in place. I was the hero. We got back about 5:00 p.m., so it made it a long weekend, and put lots of money in our pockets.

I had a few trips hauling the high school choir to Seattle for competition, and the teacher did a good job setting these trips up. We had food places lined up and motels that had plenty of parking. We got to become close and when Jim heard that I was a Santa Claus for two Christmases, he had me sneak into the Christmas concert and hide behind the choir. When it got to a certain song and a certain line, I came out from behind the choir and ran back and forth, ringing my loud bell and handing out candy as the crowd was leaving the gym. I scared the hell out of the choir since they didn't know I was behind them. Most of the band knew I was there. I did this for two years then he left and the new teacher didn't want me to do it.

I hauled a lot of basketball trips, with most of them non-eventful except when the head coach went home with his wife and left two other coaches in charge. We stopped at a little state park to use the restrooms. We realized everybody was on the bus except two cheerleaders who were still in the restroom. The coaches asked me to take off and circle the buildings, and all of a sudden, they came out running really hard trying to catch the bus, and we all laughed and stopped for them.

When I did a sports trip, it usually involved several hours, and sometimes, not getting home until after midnight. Since I had been up since 5:00 a.m. or 6:00 a.m., I'd try to catch some sleep on the bus. If it was a basketball, football, or baseball game, I would lay in one seat and prop my legs up on top of the seat across from where I was laying. My legs would get numb and wake me up about forty-five minutes later. That would tell me it was time to get up and go watch the game. If it was a sport I didn't like, I would bring a movie and watch it on the DVD player I took with me on those kinds of trips.

Track trips were always long trips since the head coach would stay to the end, and get all the times and numbers the players got. A player and I loaded the buses with other players competing in the regional playoffs in the tri-city area. We left the high school at about 11:00 a.m., and stopped at midnight at the coach's friend's pizza parlor for supper in the tri-city area. It was about 3:00 a.m., when we got back to town. It was a long day and we both made a lot of money.

Over the years at the school district, I made several trips to zoos in Tacoma and Seattle. Most of the time, the driver above me in seniority would run together since most drivers didn't want to go to Seattle. She would let me lead since she didn't know the streets as well as I did. On one Seattle Zoo trip, we had three buses and a van. I lead them to the zoo and when it was time to go home, the teacher in charge had set up reservations at a place to feed everyone. We loaded up the buses and headed out, and I had to take them down some little streets which scared the other drivers. When we got to the place to eat, they found out that a mother and daughter was missing. The teacher on their bus didn't count very well, so the van had to be sent back to look for them. The had gone to the wrong exit gate. That made for an interesting and stressful trip.

On another trip going to the sea museum downtown, I got everyone excited when I took my bus out onto a large pier, turned around in a circle, and went back out onto the street so we could park in front of the museum. I had seen a big semi-truck with a trailer make the turn so I figured it had to be safe.

Another trip to Seattle was to go to the locks where boats could get into Lake Washington from Puget Sound. It was raining, so my visibility was poor. I realized that I was in the wrong parking area, so I started back up to where I could turn around. The bad news was that there was a low wall I didn't see, so I ended up backed up onto it. Everybody got off and went to look at the locks and see it work. I got to stay there and wait for a tow turn. He lifted the back of the bus up and moved me over so I could drive out. He told me that it happened all the time. It seemed putting some signs or flags up would have helped.

I was a member of the Wenatchee Senior Center, and they had two buses to take members out to different types of shows throughout the state. I would drive for them if I wasn't driving a school bus that day. I really liked when we would go to the Mariners baseball games in Seattle. We had special parking close to the stadium and the driver and wife got in free. We had a fifty-three-passenger and a twenty-passenger bus. I took lots of trips to big skating shows and horse shows. The big bus was nice since it had a toilet on it and the smaller one didn't. Due to the cost to maintain these buses the senior Center started chartering all the trips, and sold both buses.

I hope you have enjoyed my life story, and how I started by driving a tractor, then worked my way up to different types of buses and different sizes.

About the Author

As a young boy growing up a couple miles from a small town and having a father who had cancer of the throat and heart problems we didn't have much money. All through life I worked on improving my life and proud of what I have done without any college. Working for RCA on three different programs, I was given a chance to learn a lot and given lots of responsibilities during my life as you will see in the book

Growing up outside a small town of 2,500 was a challenge. We lived about 2 miles from town with 7 1/2 acres of land with most of it in trees except about one acre around the house. We had at times a cow for milk and a pig for meat. We always had lots of chickens laying eggs. We always had big gardens which I got to weed but my mother would pick the vegetables. A neighbor boy would come over sometimes and we would sneak into the garden and eat some fresh peas out of the pod or sneak some strawberries.

In school I took a lot of classes that helped me get my first job in Alaska as a Secretary. I had a lot of fun in school and was very popular as I have a great sense of humor which I still like making people laugh. For the last 25 years I have put the Red Suit on at Christmas. I was the official Santa in Leavenworth, Wa. for five years. I rode in a horse drawn carriage into the downtown area. I would get my picture taken hundreds of times per day.

I am still very active. I am on the activities committee where we live. I do hope you enjoy the book as I have had a fun life.

Milton Keynes UK
Ingram Content Group UK Ltd.
UKHW050248280224
438578UK00003B/10